None of This Was Planned

None of This Was Planned

THE STORIES BEHIND THE STORIES

Mike McCardell

HARBOUR PUBLISHING

Harbour Publishing Co. Ltd.
P.O. Box 219, Madeira Park, BC, V0N 2H0
www.harbourpublishing.com

Cover photograph by Nick Didlick
Edited by Ian Whitelaw
Copyedited by Nicola Goshulak
Dust jacket design by Anna Comfort O'Keeffe
Text design by Mary White
Printed and bound in Canada

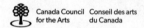  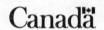

Harbour Publishing acknowledges the support of the Canada Council for the Arts, which last year invested $153 million to bring the arts to Canadians throughout the country. We also gratefully acknowledge financial support from the Government of Canada through the Canada Book Fund and from the Province of British Columbia through the BC Arts Council and the Book Publishing Tax Credit.

Library and Archives Canada Cataloguing in Publication

McCardell, Mike, 1944–, author
    None of this was planned : the stories behind the stories / Mike McCardell.

Issued in print and electronic formats.
ISBN 978-1-55017-778-7 (hardback).—ISBN 978-1-55017-779-4 (html)

    1. McCardell, Mike, 1944–. I. Title.

PN4913.M36A3 2016   C818'.602   C2016-905336-9
                                                            C2016-905337-7

I'd like to dedicate this book to Les Staff, the news director for CTV News Vancouver. Three years ago he saw my age and experience as a plus, not a negative, and hired me. It's good being a part of a happy, upbeat organization and watching the ratings soar, and it's great to be wanted. Thanks, Les.

Contents

Foreword

I can't. No way. Impossible. There is no way I can write another book.

I said that when someone said I should write another book. *"No!"* That's what I said.

Look at the facts: I am old. I am three score and ten and two. That's an old-fashioned way of counting and, when you look at it that way, that is old—at least to me.

Most importantly, I don't have any more stories to tell. I have run out of stories. There is nothing left.

I am a kid from a less desirable area of New York. Nothing was expected of me. And now I have written ten books, not counting the one with stick figures that I gave away free last year. (By the way, you can still get it.)

But I have no more stories. And look at my age! I should be sitting quietly drinking tea—only tea makes me go to the bathroom. That is a problem when you get old—okay, old*er*.

I remember seeing a poster on a wall in a bar in New York when I sneaked in with my friends when we were sixteen. We were not sup-posed to be in there before we were eighteen but the bartender said, Okay, sit in the back in the shadows and if anyone comes in with a uniform go to the bathroom and stay there.

The poster said, "I'm a member of the beer and pistol club. Drink all night and piss 'til dawn."

That was funny, I thought, even though I didn't understand it. I didn't know beer made you go to the bathroom, but it was funny because it said something we did not learn in school. Boring things were in school. I don't remember them. Exciting stuff was in the bar. An ice age later I still remember that poster.

What I also did not understand from the poster was how anyone could drink all night. I thought it was crazy. Wouldn't they get in trouble when they went home late?

Now if I drink tea after dinner I go to the bathroom in the mid-dle of the night. So I don't. And I am too old and wise to drink beer all night, or even all afternoon. Or even more than one, ever. What a state to be in.

On the other hand, I don't feel old. In fact I feel the same as when I was sixteen, except I have a lot more sense.

At sixteen I was an idiot. I dreamed of sex. I dreamed of being a hero. I didn't have sex, and nor was I a hero. Ever. I dreamed of getting through the day without screwing up in front of a girl or any friends. Those were the highest goals.

Actually, at sixteen I was deeply religious. I thought I was go-ing to be a priest or a minister—not that I went to any church. I could have been a rabbi. It didn't matter. Sneaking into a bar was not against the rules of my religion.

I prayed a great deal. God to me then was the big figure on the ceiling of the Sistine Chapel, of which I had seen a picture. He had a giant white beard and looked ticked off.

I had just returned from Germany, where I was alone much of the time. I went there when I was fourteen and came back when I was sixteen, and maybe because I was alone I found God. He was friendly.

Fourteen, fifteen and sixteen are hard years, especially when you are in a place where at first you don't understand what anyone is saying, you have no friends and there are no kids living nearby.

Our apartment building had bullet holes in the front. Germany was still digging out from years of bombing and defeat. It was a bad time.

If you've read the earlier books you'll know that I went to Germany with my mother, who worked for Radio Free Europe as a teletype operator. I know many of you have no idea what this is. Remember the sounds of clicking behind the news programs of the 1970s and the TV shows about news? Those were teletype machines. They were everywhere. They were the early version of Twitter but they made a beautiful clicking sound. My mother was a fast clicker.

Actually, almost sixty years later, I think she really went there for love. Most of us do most things because of that.

Two weeks after we arrived there a taxi pulled up in front of our apartment building and a sort of fat guy in a black suit knocked at our apartment door and my mother looked very happy.

"Go pay the driver and tell him to wait," said the fat guy to me.

He was a doctor. I knew this because my mother had told me he would visit.

I paid the driver. I knew four words in German. "Here, don't go. Thanks."

I went back into our apartment and my mother told me she was going away to Vienna for a few days with the doctor.

See? It was all for love.

After she was gone I took a long walk through the neighbourhood. The buildings still standing were mostly shells. I looked up through the bottom windows and saw the sky, six storeys up. Building after building after building.

Someone came out of the next building I passed. He ran to me, shouting, and he grabbed me and was pulling me back with him.

I said I did not understand German. He looked at me like this was impossible. Actually, I can't describe his look, but it was deep. Then he shook his head and kept pulling me.

We went through the doorway of the building he had come out of. There was no door. He led me up a broken stairway. I thought it was going to fall. I thought *I* was going to fall.

Two flights up, with nothing but empty space in the middle of the building and the sky still above, he went through a blown-out doorway into a room. I did not know how it did not fall.

He said many things to me. I understood nothing. Then in the dark he pointed to a man lying on a broken bed.

He said more things to me and then he put one of his arms under the man's arm and pointed at me to do the same.

I got on the other side and put my arm around the man. He looked at me like I was a monster. He had nothing but fear in his face.

We picked him up and I put my other arm under his legs. The man who had called me did the same and our hands grabbed each other and we lifted him and started moving toward the hole that had been a door.

The floor made a terrible groaning sound and I thought we would die. Actually, I did not consciously think that, but when I think back now I know that's the best way to explain how I felt. What was actually going through my head then was bad words, especially one, in English.

We carried him down the stairs and out the front door and put him down on the sidewalk. The man who had grabbed me thanked me.

I know what he was thinking. He knew I was American. He knew it was American bombers that had blown apart these buildings and his life. He knew that I was helping him.

I have no idea if they had lived in there since the bombing stopped or if they had moved in the night before and just decided it was not a good thing. I had no idea of anything that night and I still have no idea how it happened.

The man who stopped me thanked me again and it was clear he would be all right and I left. I walked for another hour before going back to our apartment, which was the only building on our street that was still standing.

That was my first memory of Germany. Six months later I wandered alone into Dachau. The gate was broken and open. It was the way it had been abandoned. I looked inside one of the ovens. There were rows of them. I leaned too far forward and fell, my arms went deep into ashes and bones. I said I was alone. I was not. When I walked back out past the gate I was different, I don't know how, but I do know why.

Two years later my mother came home from work and said, "We are going back to New York."

"When?"

"Next week."

This was the middle of a school year, but she looked mighty ticked off, like God in the Sistine Chapel.

Again I suspected love. Or the end of it. Still do. Don't know, of course. Will never know.

Back in New York, during the gritty times, I became Missionary Mike. As I said, I was deeply religious. I could stop fights. I could listen to kids who wanted to do really bad things to their friends and tell them not to do them—and usually they didn't. That was an amazing thing to experience. Tell someone to do something, tell them with authority, and they usually did what you said.

I listened to girls who had just been dumped by their boyfriends. I told them things would be better. And usually they were. But of course. They always are. And during it all I was still afraid of girls.

I was sixteen. Sixteen is a crazy age.

More about religion later, but now I have a new job with CTV. It was very good of them to hire me after the newly imported managers at that other place in Burnaby dumped me.

They were going in a new direction, they said. What they

meant was they wanted a youthful look. I am not youthful. I was out, totally out, after thirty-seven years, standing in the parking lot of that place in Burnaby feeling lost. Things like this happen in life. That is what gives it so much pain. I had spent more than half my life there.

A week later I was talking to the news director at CTV who asked me to come to them. He is Les Staff. He met me at a coffee shop in Lougheed mall. After we talked he asked some people sitting there if they would switch to CTV if I was on it.

I was lucky. The people he asked were wearing worn-out jackets and loose-fitting shirts. They looked like they did not go to the gym.

They said yes, of course they would switch.

If they had been in tight suits with close haircuts and perfumed faces I think they would have said, "Who?"

I got lucky. The people I like and who I do stories about wear last year's jackets.

He hired me. That is how things happen in life. First you lose by a nose, then you win by a mile. Follow that philosophy at the track and you'll die broke. Believe in it in your life and you'll live happy.

Les also told me later that he had checked the ratings and most people who start watching the news stay around to see my stories at the end.

"That's nice," I said.

"They want to see something happy," he said.

Well, gee! I know that. That's everything I believe.

He said come join us. I went, and it's been heaven. They are so nice there. I still do what I have done for so long. I still go out with no plan, no direction, nothing, and we look for something. We don't know what, but when we see it, presto! Pictures, interview, editing, writing and bingo, a smile on television.

But now I do it for someone who wants me, which is a really good feeling. If you tell someone in your family you want them, that you are happy to have them, you give them the same feeling. So what are you waiting for?

And now that I think about it, writing a new book is what I should do. Of course it is! The stories make me feel good. It's what I *want* to do. In fact, it's what I *will* do. So you are stuck with me for one more.

What I tell everyone, in the talks I give, in books and on television, is that the stories you gather are precious and exciting. Some are dramatic, some are less so. They can be funny or sweet or terrible. It doesn't matter. Whatever they are, they are wonderful. We all have them, we can share them and they are free. You have them for as long as you have your mind, and at some time later in your life they will be the most precious things you have.

To keep your mind, I think, is luck. To put things in it that you treasure is simple. You just go out and search for them.

You can tell the stories, remember them, smile at them, and when you go somewhere that you haven't been for a while you can suddenly say to yourself or someone else, "You know what happened here?" And then you tell it. "I met someone who . . ." The place and the memory come alive.

It's better than collecting bottle caps or stamps or stocks (which can leave you feeling so, so ill). Stories are better than money, better than whiskey or wine (and eventually you should be too wise for those). They are almost as good as new love, which leads to new memories no matter how old you are.

That's it. In here are more of my treasures, the stories that I have accidentally stumbled upon. This is the fun part of collecting: sharing the collection. I'll give you mine first. You write back and give me yours.

So I will now close my eyes and see what I remember. One new book coming up!

ps: If you would like to read last year's free, yes free, book, go to mike.mccardell@bellmedia.ca and I'll send you a copy. It doesn't have covers like this book, and you can't hold it, but heck it's free and it may make you want to buy more of these real books, even the ones I wrote before this, and that would make me and Harbour Publishing very happy. And by the way, Harbour is made up of very nice people who are giving writers on the West Coast a chance to be published. It's a chance they wouldn't have anywhere else.

Back in Time and Space: The Taxi Garage

*E*veryone back then went to work at sixteen and gave half their paycheque to their mothers. And I mean everyone. Try that now. I got a job in a taxicab garage.

"You start tomorrow, kid, and be on time." That was the boss with a cigar and a fat belly. He did not look like the teachers in school.

I worked every day three p.m. to seven p.m., all day Saturday and half a day on Sunday. I had every other Sunday off. The fact that school ended at three and I started at three was a problem. I ran very fast.

"You're ten minutes late," said the boss. "You get docked a half-hour."

That meant that for working fifty minutes I would make fifty cents.

What I did was pump gas into a fleet of cabs that ended their day shift at three. I pumped the gas, opened the hood, checked the oil, opened the caps on the batteries (yes, batteries had caps that unscrewed and inside was water that had to be refilled), and then the worst part: the radiator. On a hot day, after ten or twelve hours of stop and go driving, the radiator was like a kettle that was hissing on a stove, and the water inside had to be checked.

A big rag went on top of the cap and with all my weight I pushed down and turned it so slowly it barely moved but enough to let out the steam.

"Please don't blow, please."

Open it too much and it would. Scalding hot water would shoot up into the rag and onto me.

"Please don't."

"Hey, kid, hurry up with that radiator. I gotta go."

That from the driver still smoking a cigar, with the gasoline pump an arm's stretch away. But almost every driver had something to say—weird, strange, scary, erotic—about someone who had been in the back seat.

"He was gonna blow up the world. He said that."

"He brought his poodle. A guy had a poodle. Can you imagine that?"

"This lady was changing her clothes. I tried not to look. But she was. So I looked."

And after the last cab came in I swept the vast garage floor. Then I went home stinking of gas and oil and did my homework—or not.

"You should wash," said my mother.

But I was too tired. I went to bed and thought about the things the cabbies had said.

How I Got to Do What I Am Doing

I know I have told you some of this before, but that was long ago.

I did badly in school. I had trouble reading, so they ignored me. I know others who had trouble hearing. They didn't respond to teachers and so they were put in the back of the classroom. It happens.

But, lucky me, I was in a classroom where the teacher's only job was to keep us quiet while he read newspapers. He brought in the tabloids—the *New York Daily News* and the *Mirror*. They were both filled with crime and scandal.

They were written at a sixth-grade level. Their stories were exciting and short. This I could read. And when I got hold of the newspapers, I did.

Right there, right there in that classroom, I decided I wanted to be a reporter and meet the people in those stories. I didn't care about the nobility of journalism. I didn't want to be a writer. I just wanted to hang out with Two Finger Louis and Shotgun Sally and their friends who filled the pages of the tabloids between ads for "I'll paint any car any colour for $24.99."

I was surprised, actually awed, when I found out that ads like that were placed there to help criminals. Of course honest people sometimes get their cars repainted; sometimes, not often, but occasionally. Mostly, though, painting quick and cheap was one way of covering up a stolen car. Right there in the newspaper was an education. It was more useable knowledge than geometry.

None of us in that classroom graduated in June with the other kids. It was the following February that we were released.

My mother met me later. She had a six-pack of beer and two ham sandwiches to celebrate.

"What are you going to do now?" she asked.

"I want to work for a newspaper."

"Well then, go to a newspaper."

Such a good idea. Why didn't I think of it? She gave me a subway token.

I got off the train at Times Square where the *New York Times* was and I went to the personnel office. This was not a tabloid but it was where the train stopped. They offered me a job as an outdoor messenger. It was cold in February.

I walked across town and passed the *Daily News*. It was purely by accident. I didn't know I was heading there. I saw a carving in stone over the front doors:

"He made so many of them."

There were carvings of people below that. I knew it was from the Bible and, again, I was very religious. I went inside. They offered me a job as an indoor messenger working in the mailroom. I took it.

I had no writing qualifications, but I found I liked being in the newsroom, the city room as it was called, so I started hanging out there while I was supposed to be working in the mailroom.

I started changing typewriter ribbons, getting coffee and beer and inhaling the excitement of people on deadlines yelling, "How many dead?"

After a while I asked to be transferred from the boring mailroom to the exciting, yelling city room. Maybe they could sense my desire or maybe they just needed someone else to sharpen pencils, but I got the job. The same pay as the taxi garage, one dollar an hour, with an extra fifty cents a day for working nights, and nights were what I worked.

I was lucky, because if you want to be around crime and excitement as well as beer and deadlines and shouting, the night shift is where it's at. Until I came to Canada I never worked days again.

I stayed there eleven years and I went from bottom copy boy to top copy boy and then bottom reporter to, well, not so bad reporter. I was doing what I had dreamed of, mostly because of a subway token and a walk across town.

There is a lesson in that. Do what your mother says and you will be all right.

Pizza for the Pigs

It is hard to write this because my good friends might be criminals, although they are not really. They have six guinea pigs. And if you counted more than six it is only because you could not count accurately. It is your fault. Guinea pigs can slip in and out of a counter's field of vision very fast.

"I didn't count that one yet."

"Yes, you did. That one over there you counted twice."

"Did not. They are different ones."

"No, this is a different one. You already counted the one that just came out from under the sofa."

"Let's start again."

And in the end they have six; not eight or ten or twelve or thirteen or fifteen as some people who have no idea how to count have wrongly stated.

If they ever did have that many then they would be in violation of the guinea pig law, which says you can only have six guinea pigs no matter how much you love them—and the pig owners *do* love them. So they only have six.

Now these six guinea pigs roam free in their house. Please don't hold up your refined nose at that. When you love your pigs as much as they do, they say, the pigs should be free.

Their names—that would be the names of the pigs' owners not the pigs—are Ingrid and Bob. I will not tell you their last names because the guinea pig authorities could track them down, and it is possible that the authorities might make a mistake in their counting, but I will tell you that Ingrid is a famous editorial cartoonist and Bob is a well-known pianist.

I'm not going to tell you the names of all the pigs, despite the fact that over the last twenty-five years Bob and Ingrid have kept a list of every pig they have ever owned, fed, nurtured and brought back to health with expensive vet bills.

They have kept the names in a notebook from which some pages are falling out and some are held in by tape. They keep the names because they have never *ever* repeated a name. They have more than seventy names in the book.

They didn't always have more than one pig but one day, after their one pig died, they went to a nice pet shop and came home with one that they didn't know was, well, you can guess the rest. She was pregnant, and then they had more than one guinea pig. Now they *only* have girls in fur coats.

Anyway, a little while ago a problem came up in their world of pigs. One of the restaurants Bob played in on Davie Street ended its "music with dinner" program. That was unfortunate. The big problem for Bob was that he had been taking home the leftover pizza crusts for the pigs. They like pizza crusts. It doesn't matter whether the pizza is anchovy or pepperoni, it's the crusts they covet.

Now the six pigs (that's all, and please don't ask again) had been without pizza for several weeks and, except for the fact that they are rather plump, they were starving, at least for pizza. You know the feeling.

Bob and Ingrid decided to have a party at their home to make up for the lack of music with dinner on Davie Street. Bob invited all the singers and musicians who had had impromptu sessions with him. He invited anyone who could play an instrument, anyone who could sing or anyone who could listen to the first two categories.

Just one request. Please bring pizza.

Forty people came and they all brought pizza. Some brought two. There were pizzas in the oven and on a table in the kitchen and piled on dishes next to the sink. There were pizzas on top of pizzas with more pizzas on top of them.

There were people who had never been there before and their first reaction was, "That's a lot of pizzas."

Their second reaction was, "You still have your Christmas tree up!" This was the middle of January.

There is no logical point in taking down a Christmas tree when the guinea pigs can frolic below it through the winter with needles falling on their heads. As I keep saying, these are well-loved guinea pigs.

A friend gave Ingrid and Bob a fire extinguisher to stand next to the tree but they have delayed taking down their tree after many, many Christmases and many, many pigs have delightedly played with the needles.

The third reaction, when they stepped into the kitchen, was, "What is that?"

It is a three-storey condo for guinea pigs, a condo with an open door policy and a thick pile of hay to jump into when they go out.

They are happy pigs.

"Do they really run free?" the first-timers ask.

To which Ingrid replies, "Would you lock them up?" What she means is, "If you would you can leave."

There was music with piano and drums and singing and pizza and wine and pigs squeaking and it was a fine night. That is when I sat in a cozy chair with guinea pigs sniffing my shoes.

I tried counting them. Four, five, my eyes started closing, sleepy, too much pizza, but there, under that chair, six. Just like the rules say. Even with my eyes closed I can guarantee you I counted just six for absolute sure.

Ingrid does a lot for her pigs. She has invented a guinea pig wheelchair for the older ones who sometimes lose the use of their rear legs. It consists of the soft sole of an old beach thong, some hook-and-loop straps and a couple of wheels. Attach it to the crippled pigs and they can run for pizza with the rest.

And because some guinea pigs suffer with malocclusion, where the top and bottom teeth don't meet as they should, Ingrid has made a sling for their tiny jaws and it solves the problem, although I can't explain how.

Mind you, the pigs don't get all this free. They work for it. In the summer they get put out in a giant cage with no bottom and their job is to mow the grass, which they do while fertilizing the ground for more grass to grow.

It was a perfect arrangement until Ingrid and Bob put the pigs outside their fenced-in yard to cut the city-owned grass. Someone who thought this was cruel called the SPCA.

When the officials checked they found the six, yes just six (at that moment), six pigs as happy as pigs in grass and well protected by the cage. The officials gave them an official okay and Ingrid put a sign on her fence behind the cage saying that this is an SPCA-approved ecological pig party turning grass to food to fertilizer that becomes grass—so please don't complain.

They also have a cat but I don't know how.

The neat thing about knowing Ingrid and Bob is learning how to count to six.

Some time later the story of the guinea pigs mowing the grass was on CTV. Cameraman Jazz Sanghera and I were approaching the house, which is in a secret location because we don't want people who can't count going there.

"Can you count to six?" I asked.

He said he had been to India once this year to visit relatives, and to Vancouver Island twice last month to visit his parents, and last week he played golf three times. "I think I can do it," he said.

Jazz is always upbeat, and having someone like that to work with is wonderful. Employers, take note. Find people who love their family, are active in some way not connected to their work, and can count.

"Wow!" said Jazz when he went into Ingrid and Bob's fenced-off private backyard. "That's a lot of guinea pigs."

"No, just six," I said. "Go ahead, count them."

"One, two."

"Wait a minute. You counted the first one twice."

Then two of the ground huggers went behind the organic chard, which is grown mainly for them.

"One, two, three."

"Wait!" I said, again. "Number three was just slipping into a tunnel. That was a miscount."

Ingrid makes long pup-tent tunnels around her yard for her friends to hide in when the nasty birds that eat her friends are flying around, and obviously you can't count them when they are inside— or was that one outside?

"Six," Jazz said. "You're right."

Later that day he played golf. "The way I counted it I had six under par," he told me.

The Truck with the Wishing Well

Most of the stories are funny. As I said a while ago, we travel in circles while looking for something that is straight ahead. That is either funny or stupid, but it works.

"No one is out," I said. It's raining. There's no one but dog walkers. I like dogs and I like dog walkers, but I do not like people walking dogs while I am looking for someone doing something that can go on television and time is passing and the weather is getting worse and I know the editor has given up and gone to lunch and all the world is falling apart.

"What is *that?*"

"What is what?"

Doesn't matter who says what, the cameraman or me. What's important is it was said.

"*That!*"

Going the other way on Main Street is not an art car but an art *truck*. I have done stories on art cars, those idiotic creations of brilliant artists who use cars as canvases and weld stuff—dolls, hub-caps, pictures, any stuff—onto their cars.

But this is an old postal truck: big, awkward, swaying, beautiful. And going the other way.

"I'll get it," said the cameraman, Scott Connorton.

A U-turn, an illegal U-turn on Main Street, and the chase is on.

One block, two blocks, three.

Please don't be going to Burnaby or Coquitlam or Maple Ridge. Please.

A light turns red. No, actually it is already red, but I jump out and run up, in the rain, with the traffic, to the passenger side of the truck. I don't have time to go to the other side.

And staring at me through the passenger window is . . . a witch. No, a mannequin. No, a hairy woman with her fingernails out-stretched. Then the light turns green, the truck pulls away and I run back to Scott and his SUV with cameras and gear in the back. It is basically an outlandish movable studio on the hunt for outlandishly strange oddities to photograph.

"We'll get him this time," he says.

Scott has a house full of children whom he's trying to raise in a good, civic-minded, law-abiding way.

Yellow light, almost red, gotta stop. Gotta.

Zoom. Don't tell his children.

Red light. Stop!

I run up to the driver's side and, wonderful, it is a *woman!*

I love women, professionally. They are so much better on televi-sion than men. They are alive and talkative and funny and touching and just plain neat.

But there are so few of them out where you can find them. After doing this job for a long, long time, I have found most of the creatures on the street available for television's instant fame are men. Darn! The women are home cooking or cleaning or raising and helping others grow, or they are at work before they go home to cook and do the other stuff. And that's just the beginning of the things that they do. The men are out, not cooking or cleaning or raising and helping others grow. Even if you are one of the good guys who do help, 90 percent of the stories I've done have men as the main character because men are generally out and about and women aren't.

Despite all the advances in equality, men don't do an equal amount of anything and women do more and women are home, or working and then home, and I get stuck with men.

But now, there's a woman behind the wheel.

"Hello, we're from CTV, we do stories, could you pull over?"

I did not add the "please" that was screaming in my head. I didn't have time for that.

"Yes," she said.

Oh heavens. If I've been praying it has been answered.

I get back in Scott's truck and we follow her around the corner. Then I jump out. He looks for parking and I run. Yes, I am ancient but I run, just across the street but I still run. When a little kid sees a puddle and he wants to jump in it, he runs to it. That's me. I run to her side door.

She slides it open and says what most women say, "Can I first put on my makeup?"

My God! First of all, thank you God for not making me a woman (because I can't stand makeup), and second, thank you God for letting her say that.

"Can we take a picture of you putting on your lipstick?"

"Yes."

How lucky can you get? Most of the news of the world is pictures of explosions, fires, shootings and politicians making phony aggressive gestures with their fingers. We have lipstick.

Scott parks and comes up to the truck with his camera. She is turning her lips red. My gosh. A picture of a woman putting on lipstick. Unbelievably expensive commercials are made of this, but the commercials take days to film and Scott has it in ten seconds. Women will understand what a remarkable feat this is.

I am so happy I could again jump, except we are on a street just off Main in the rain and traffic is squeezing by.

"Is this truck yours? Did you do it?"

Please say yes.

"Yes."

"Could you show us around?"

"Yes."

Give me a church with some candles to light.

"I'll hold my umbrella over your head," I say, because I don't want her to change her mind.

Then I realize if I hold up an umbrella we can't see her. So I fold up my umbrella and hold the dripping wet nylon in my dripping wet fingers while she gets out and I don't hold the dripping wet thing over her head like I had just promised.

Please don't notice, I think.

I finally introduce myself and Scott. That should have been first but everything is happening at once so this is still first. "Michelle," she says, or over the noise of the traffic I think that is what she said.

"This is my cup holder and this is the wishing well."

She shows us the cup holder on the outside of her truck, not the inside but the outside, which is a brilliant idea. You have to put your cup somewhere while you open the door, right?

And then the wishing well. It is a . . . wishing well. How do you describe a wishing well? It's a small wishing well on the side of her truck with a little fairy beside it.

It is half-filled with coins and there is a sign next to it painted on the truck that says, "If you take anything out of the well it is bad karma, and you don't want that."

So the well has coins in it.

"I lived in this for three years while I drove across America and Canada singing and spreading joy."

"Will you sing now?"

I know most people who say they do something, when I ask

them to do that something, they say, "No! Can't now. Not now. I won't sound good. I need to warm up. Maybe later."

She said yes.

And she sang, so beautifully. Thank you.

And what about the department-store dummy in the side window that scared the socks off me?

"She is my friend who tells the future," said Michelle.

Then she had to go to work. She is a chauffeur for a limo company. She drives a conservative car looking professional with her lipstick and incredibly good driving skills. If they only knew.

But we know. And so do you. All because we stopped someone to ask if we could take a picture. You should try it—but not in traffic.

Now the PS.

We are all human. We all make mistakes. The editor, Vinh Nguyen, was listening to me record the words that go with the story: "Michelle decorated the truck herself," I said.

"Are you sure that's her name?" he asked.

Whoops. How can I, with more years of experience than he's been alive, say, "I think so"?

Double whoops, because there is no way I can check. I don't have a phone number, I don't have the place she works except it is a limo company. I could start calling all of them and ask if they have a woman who drives a strange truck working for them. And even if they didn't say they can't release private information it would still be seven or eight p.m. before I got through.

Vinh said he remembered another story about the woman and her truck done several years ago. How did he remember? I don't know. And how did it stick in his mind that her name might not be Michelle.

He did a good deal of searching to find the other story then said: "It might be Marilyn."

"Oh, God, yes, of course. That *is* what she said," I said in my excited, humble, suddenly-brought-back-to-reality voice.

I changed the name in the story to Marilyn.

Vinh is a nice guy who knows computers inside out, and editing and being friendly, and obviously he has a wonderful memory.

How did he happen to come to this job?

This is where the story takes a dramatic change of direction from funny and happy to serious and important.

His father was one of the boat people who escaped from Vietnam. He paid someone a hefty price to get on an old, crowded ship and hope some other country would take him in.

He left a home ripped apart by war for the sake of the future of his son and wife, who stayed behind.

Canada took him in. In that, he was lucky, but easy was not part of his life. It took six years for him to get permits to have his family join him.

I wasn't there, but at Vinh's wedding a year ago he gave a toast to his parents, in Vietnamese, that made them cry, along with everyone else, most of whom did not understand his words but knew what he was saying.

In a roundabout way his father escaping and being taken in by a new country resulted in a woman's name being correct on the air. That is a minor thing—except, of course, for the woman—but in a major way Vinh's father, with the help of Canada, gave him a good life and made this country better.

Now Canada is taking refugees from other wars. Some people are opposed to this because they say we have trouble finding housing for people already living here. And why should they be helped with government money when so many others need it? And why can't they go somewhere else? And, although no one actually says it, they are different from us.

It's not unlike the sorry tale of the SS *Komagata Maru*, a ship that reached these shores a hundred years ago only to be turned away.

You know the story, I'm sure. I told it in my last book, *Haunting Vancouver: A Nearly True History*, so you must know it. The ship was carrying 376 men from Punjab in India, men who were citizens of the British Commonwealth and had a legal right to live in Canada, but when it tried to dock in Vancouver it was refused permission. The city's white folks, who outnumbered everyone else here, said they did not want brown-skinned people with turbans moving in.

The white folks had already made up a crazy law that said immigrants had to come here directly from their country of origin without stopping anywhere else. Passengers on ships coming from Europe could do this, but it was impossible for a ship coming from India. It had to stop for coal.

"Sorry folks, you did not come directly so you can't dock," the men were told.

One of the white men who would not let them dock was a former national hero, hockey star Cyclone Taylor. When the ship arrived here he was an immigration officer who later became the Immigration Commissioner for BC and the Yukon and received the Order of the British Empire for his services. "You know the rules," he said. "We have to go by the rules."

Those on the ship were not expecting a band to greet them when they arrived, but what they got was a fleet of men in small boats surrounding them singing "White Canada Forever," a popular song back then. They had almost no food and no water, but, "Sorry folks, you can't get it from us."

For two months they pleaded to be allowed to land. In the end they were forced to return to Calcutta, but now they were seen as traitors and a threat to British rule in India. When they landed, the police tried to arrest several of them, and in the riot that followed, nineteen of them were shot before they could leave the dock, and many others were imprisoned.

It was a shameful chapter in Canada's history, but it took the government almost a century to apologize.

These are not happy stories, but they are important and they have to be included.

Another story about refugees has nothing to do with BC or Canada, but it I found it so sad and so important I felt you should know about it.

It was in an obituary in the *New York Times* that I read on January 24, 2016, and it was about the death of a man two years earlier. The *New York Times* had only just learned about it, but it was important enough to still run the obituary two years late.

The man was David Stoliar. He died in Oregon and there was only a small notice in a local paper when he died. His story almost vanished but someone, somehow, in the *Times* newsroom recognized his name and the paper published the story.

In 1942 David Stoliar was a refugee, a boat person. He was one of 790 mostly Romanian Jews trying to escape the death sentence imposed on them by the Nazis.

They each begged and borrowed $1,000, a gigantic amount, to pay a rip-off artist for a place on an old ship, very much as refugees are doing today. As the *Times* story said, they were "crowded into a squalid, leaky former cattle boat with bunks stacked 10 high, little food or fresh water, no kitchen and only eight toilets." There were no life preservers.

They, like all refugees, were desperate.

They wanted to get to Palestine, a safe place for Jews. Shortly after leaving Romania the engine on the ship died. A passing tug boat captain offered to fix it but only in exchange for the wedding rings of all the passengers.

He repaired the engine but three days later as the ship neared Turkey it broke down again. The Turks, who were neutral in the war, towed it close to the shore, but would not allow anyone off and would not fix it for fear of offending either Britain or Germany.

Then Britain, which had control of Palestine, refused to allow the scared, hungry refugees to go to Palestine for fear of offending the Arabs.

For seventy-one days the passengers were kept waiting, tied in one spot in the ocean while the Turks deliberated on what to do.

Finally the Turks cut the anchor chain, towed the ship out into the open ocean and left it to drift.

The next day a Soviet submarine saw it and, following their orders to sink all neutral ships so they would not aid Germany, fired a torpedo into the side of this ship filled with refugees.

In an instant the ship exploded. Those who were not killed outright were left screaming in a freezing ocean with no life preservers. One by one they sank below the water, too tired and cold to go on.

David Stoliar, who was young and strong and was able to hold onto a piece of wooden decking, was the only survivor. When he was picked up by a passing ship and returned to Turkey the Turkish authorities held him in prison for six weeks, apparently to keep him from telling any possible reporter what had happened.

He eventually made it to Palestine and joined the British Army's Jewish Brigade. Later he moved to the US.

For decades he said nothing about it. No one cared.

In 2001 a Canadian filmmaker did a documentary about the ship. That was when the *New York Times* first heard about David Stoliar and prepared his obituary. David Stoliar died in 2014. The obituary ran in 2016.

The importance of the story is not the two-year delay. The importance is in knowing that refugees are like you, and me, and when we need help, "No!" is not a good thing to hear.

Because Vinh's father heard "Welcome to Canada," Vinh and his father and mother and family have made this a better Canada. And that is an even better story than the wishing well on the truck.

Period.

God—in a Hard Hat

*B*ack to religion. Now there's a taboo subject, but I started talking about it at the beginning so let's go back to it.

Religion is big in my life. God is big. Of course God is big. Look at all those cathedrals and Sunday morning television shows where we are told God lives. Many of them are bigger than the great outdoors, which is a far better place for chatting with the Force, which is a really good Star Wars way of describing God.

As I told you, when I was young I had heavy duty religion. Then I read the Bible. Reading is not a big thing in my life. It is hard to concentrate on piles of words (you can read about that in my free book—remember, just ask and it's yours) but I struggled through much of the holy book and said to myself, "Wait a minute. Just wait. It looks like someone is blaming women for most of men's problems. Don't ask me to justify that." That was the way it looked to me—and that was just in the first couple of chapters.

Eve was not guilty, and when I figured out what the serpent was

I didn't think it was even Eve getting tempted by him. It was him doing what he does naturally and then blaming it on Eve.

It was like saying, "She's only a teenager and she got herself pregnant. Shame on her."

Huh?

And then I read more of the Old Testament and I found endless stories of smiting and slaying, and then endless stories of multiplying and begetting.

So we have lots of smiting and multiplying and slaying and begetting. Sex and violence, just like the newspapers.

The way I saw it—and this has nothing to do with the Church or theology or basic beliefs, it is just the way I saw it—a couple of monks were ordered to write the history of the world, from the beginning.

One monk says to the other monk, "Sex is bad. We are not supposed to have it so it must be bad."

The other monk says, "You're right. We only need praying and oatmeal. Although I think about it sometimes."

The first one says, "That's a sin. Thinking about it is a sin. And without women we would not have the thinking and we would not have the sin. So it must be her fault."

The other says, "Eve started it all, blame her."

"But it was Adam who did that sinful thing with her."

"Well we can't blame him. Guys have to stick together."

"We could say she started it after she was tempted by something. That would make her weak, unlike guys, who are strong."

"Tempted with what?"

"You know what."

"But we can't say that."

"So call it a snake. It looks like a snake."

"But snakes aren't bad. They eat the mice that eat our oatmeal."

"So call it a serpent."

"What's that?"

"A snake with a bad name."

"Good idea. We will have Eve tempted by a serpent."

"What does she do when she's tempted?"

"Well, you know. She gives in."

"But we can't say that, we're monks. And besides, the chief monk would have us in itchy shirts for a month if we wrote that."

"Okay, have her offer an apple to Adam."

"What's an apple?"

This is Palestine, Israel, the desert, long ago. There were no apples.

"I read about them in Dr. Oz's book on health. You should eat one every day."

"Isn't Dr. Oz coming much later in time."

"No, every age has one."

"So according to him we should we have lunch with Eve and eat apples?"

"Don't go there. That's a sin."

Remember, this is my interpretation of how I read Genesis. It has nothing to do with theological schools.

"We'll have Eve offer Adam a bite of her apple. And that will start the world in eternal decline."

"But I thought apples were good for you!"

"Now they are but then they weren't. It's like everything—good one year, bad the next. Like wine. Last year it was good for you, this year it's not."

"Is that true? About wine?"

"Don't worry. This is still last year, when it was good."

And so religions multiplied, and soon Protestants and Catholics were killing each other. Sunnis and Shiites did the same. Christians killed atheists. Buddhists in Mongolia, who kill nothing, killed Muslims. And the poor Jews were on everyone's hit list.

In my view, this is not good.

With the help of newspapers I got to seeing that everyone killed everyone else. Whites and blacks in America did it. Germans and Americans did it. Russians and Americans, Vietnamese and Americans, Afghans and Americans . . . Wait a minute. Is there is a pattern here?

In my world God likes everyone, and I like that.

I personally get my connection through holes in the clouds. I've told you this before, but when I need help I look for a break in the cloudy sky and ask. If it's raining I forget about holes and just hammer right through the clouds.

It works just as well, and since I believe things will be okay after that, they *are* okay.

Simple. Undeniable.

Please don't argue with me. Don't criticize. Don't say I am crazy or naïve or unbalanced or desperately looking for something impossible. Okay, say it if you want, but it works, and that is all I need.

I think God is everything. The sky, the worms, the past, the future, evolution, us, all creation and that metaphysical stuff we don't know about. I don't think God cares if god is written with a capital G or not. I think God wears coveralls and a hard hat and work boots, and carries a pencil and a notebook for recording recipes for chocolate chip cookies and taking notes on what's going on.

Someday he will write a real Divine Comedy and maybe Harbour will publish it.

And there is only one rule in my religion, not ten. No sermons, no rituals, just one rule: be nice, especially when it is hard to be nice.

That's it. Do that and everything will be okay.

Remember that "Desiderata" thing? If you don't, please Google it. Everyone should read it.

"You are a child of the universe, no less than the trees and the stars; you have a right to be here."

And remember Joni Mitchell's epoch-defining song "Woodstock," in which she tells us we are stardust?

That's it. Nothing more, except that for a while we stir up the dust and then we go back to being it. So really there is not much worth worrying about.

When you are looking for something wonderful look for a hole in the clouds. After that you will get what you believe, if you believe it.

Go back to one of my earlier books and read about Reilly. If you know who I am talking about, well then, you know. I don't have to explain it.

If you don't, he was an autistic ten-year-old who believed he would catch a fish where there were no fish.

"You can do anything you want to do, if you believe it," he said.

He changed my life.

I'll tell you about him again a little later.

One Pond, One Word

*W*e could find nothing, as happens so often, but it's like life or prospecting for gold or hunting for a recipe. You have to keep looking until you find it. If you find it right away you are lucky, but then you think you can always find things right away and you stop trying if you don't. Then you don't get what you want—and that's a well-known fact. The rule if you want something is don't quit. Simple.

We could find nothing. Cameraman Todd Gilchrist and I had done the Stanley Park–Main Street–East Hastings route and nothing was jumping up saying, "Put me on television."

We had done side streets, alleys and alcoves off alleys. Then Todd started heading east. The PNE. There is always something there.

"After we find something I'll show you the fishing pond," I said.

"What pond?"

Ahhh, I think. Another person who does not know.

This was one of the fiercest of civic battles about twenty years ago. A group of enthusiastic environmentalists wanted the historic Pacific National Exhibition bulldozed into oblivion.

"We want a park for our neighbourhood, not a bunch of rides and hot dog stands for others that is used only two weeks a year and that brings all those people who pay to park in other people's backyards, which is a source of annoyance."

That was one heck of a protest chant.

Hundreds of thousands of others wanted to keep the PNE because it is one of the last remaining real country fairs with rides and hot dog stands and they wouldn't know it was the end of summer without it.

In the end, compromise.

Half the PNE was bulldozed and turned into a park, and if you have never seen it (as most people haven't), it is beautiful. It was designed to look the way it looked before any folks with white skin and sharp axes showed up.

Maybe it does and maybe it doesn't, but it doesn't matter. It is beautiful and peaceful and full of birds and trout, with the fresh, sweet air turning into a calm homemade quilt that comforts everyone there.

On the other side of the pond is East Hastings, with traffic and sirens and people and noise.

I saw two women walking toward the park.

"Hurry, stop, park. I'm going to find out what they are doing and do a story about it, and if I fail I am going to bang my head against your hubcaps," I said to Todd.

Maybe I didn't say exactly that, but it was close because it was 12:30 and, in my idyllic life, worry was setting in.

They were two friends, Jill and Jane. They were both retired nurses, they had some time to kill before meeting friends for lunch and they were bird watchers, so what place better to wait? That's what they said.

I agree, I said.

There really was nothing to do a story about. No beginning, no end, and no middle between the no anythings at either end.

The women recognized a few birds and then said they had to go.

But Todd had taken pictures of their visit, and of the birds on the water and reflections of trees in the water. Each time a bird landed on the pond the reflections shimmered.

Okay, I will write something nice about the pond, about the passing sirens, about the peace and beauty and calmness—or I really will bang my head against Todd's hubcaps.

Back at the TV station I worked with James Buck. He is a brilliant editor. The others are brilliant too, and I will tell you about them, but today it was James.

"No story?" he said.

"No," I said.

"So just pictures?" he said.

"I will say nice things," I said.

And I did. I talked about calmness and peace and birds. I said that coming here was like going to an art gallery, seeing all the beautiful pictures. I said the best things I could say.

Then came the end, the last line, the most important one.

"I've said everything I can say," I said.

We were looking at the shimmering water with a reflection of the trees.

"Tomorrow, a new picture in the same gallery," I said.

He said nothing. He just shook his head ever so slowly.

"Every day a new portrait of nature," I said.

He shook his head.

"So what?" I said, just a tiny bit exasperated.

"How about, 'Tomorrow, same canvas, new painting,'" he said.

"Okay, that will do," I said, and then I said it into the microphone. How could I admit that was the best line in the entire story? It was the best line I had heard all day. Maybe all week. And *I* was supposed to be the writer, not James.

I was happy to finish. The story was nice, I thought. Not great, because there was no story, but okay.

The next day I saw the news director walking to work as I was leaving. This was not good. I should not finish before he starts. On the other hand I'm sure he was at an early morning meeting where important things were discussed concerning the later morning meeting. News directors and executives often reveal their brilliance at meetings. Shoot for that position if you get the chance.

"That story on the pond was beautiful," he said.

OK. I will stop walking and listen because this news director is obviously super brilliant.

"Thank you."

"The writing was perfect," he said.

A bus hitting me in the back would not have moved me more. Doesn't matter how old you are or how long you have done something, a compliment is like a snowdrop in winter. A wonderful surprise.

"Thanks."

"Especially that line, 'same canvas, new painting.'"

"Oh," I said. What I was thinking was: hurt, darn, pain, bummer, embarrassment—or simply an expected kick in the something or other.

"Well, I've got to tell you . . ." I started to say.

"Gotta go," he said. "Late."

"But . . ."

I know he thought I was going to say something humble, like "I'm glad you liked it. Thank you for noticing. You are a thoughtful boss."

He didn't want to hear that, so he was gone.

The next day I waited for him to be alone so I could tell him who wrote the line. He was never alone.

I stopped by James's editing room, James the editor who is not paid as a writer.

"You know what happened?" I asked him, and I told him the story of the last line.

He held up a finger by his lips. "Shhh. Don't tell."

The moral: editors, whoever they are, the ones who fix news stories or books or suggest ways you can live better, like wives and mothers and friends, are the most valuable folks you will ever meet. Listen to them, and thank them.

PS: The pond is beautiful. Go visit. Every minute you will see the same canvas with new paintings.

PPS: A week later I finally got to tell the news director. He laughed. The story behind the story is always the best one.

Two Women, One Stupid Question

I don't know if they were a couple or not. My first thought was, "Yes, of course," but that is stereotyping. My second thought was, "Don't stereotype."

After we left and got back in his truck it was the first thing the cameraman asked.

When I stepped into the edit room it was the first thing the editor asked.

After it was on the air it was the first thing a friend of mine asked in an email.

And it had nothing to do with the story.

Here are the facts: cameraman Gary Rutherford and I were driving on a side street in Vancouver. He had just finished telling me about his dog getting sick on New Year's Eve and having to take it to an emergency animal hospital. The dog survived. His wallet was near death. Not the kind of problem you want to have on New Year's Eve.

Then we saw a woman sweeping her front walkway.

"That looks beautiful," I said, because it truly was. A person doing something is always beautiful. It is the other end of doing nothing.

Gary waved. She waved back.

"Stop," I said, as though he would do anything else.

I got out and while Gary was getting his camera from the back of his mountain-climbing vehicle, I said hello to the white-haired woman with a smile.

She said hello. Her name was Shirley and we were off to a good start.

Standing near to the straw of her broom was a sign stuck in the soil of her garden: "Come Up to the Porch and Take a Look."

"Want to see my castle before I take it down?" she asked.

Well yes, of course. Thank you. We stood on her porch and looked through her front window at a castle. Shirley pointed to the queen on horseback crossing a drawbridge. The tiny regal plastic figure was waving at us.

She was entering a mammoth glittering silver fairy tale. Shirley told us the castle was made of Pringles cans and the middles from rolls of toilet paper and paper towel, all covered with aluminum foil: a giant, precise, beautiful, royal undertaking.

It was as wide as my arms could stretch and half as tall as me. Beautiful.

Then the front door opened and out onto the porch stepped another woman, also white haired and smiling.

"This is Marilyn," said Shirley.

Marilyn was wearing slippers.

There was only one thought I had, and it was a pure, golden thought, because two people who are the same gender living together is now as common as two raindrops falling together. But I had the thought. Not the question, but the thought.

"Shirley makes them and then gives them away," said Marilyn.

Immediately the story was perfect: art, kindness, Christmas. All we had to do was get close-up pictures of the queen's men on horseback following her into the silver world and pictures of the turrets and windows and everything.

Marilyn disappeared into the house saying she had things to do and Shirley told us that some of the plastic figures around the castle belonged to her mother and she, Shirley, was eighty-five, so the pieces are quite old.

She was happy. I was ecstatic. Gary was taking pictures.

We left with a happy goodbye and a thank you.

Inside his truck Gary asked, "Do you think they are a couple?"

"Well, I don't know. They sure are nice. They looked happy together."

In the edit room Greg Novik looked at the pictures of them and said, "Such a nice couple."

Greg is a powerful, wise man who has conversations about everything: how the world is run, the history of television, the beauty of jewellery and planting squash. He never talks about his personal life, except to occasionally mention his partner. That's all, nothing else.

"Nice couple," he said again, looking at the women.

One of the first rules in television is a minute thirty. It's right up there with facts and information.

That means stories cannot be longer than ninety seconds. This is a good rule because:

1) The attention span of many who watch is about ninety seconds. Please don't take offence. This is a well-known fact told to me by someone who knows such things.

2) There are only sixty minutes in an hour-long news show and if you take away the time for commercials there are only forty-four minutes left. And if you take away the time the anchors are on the air making you wish you were as smart and knowledgeable and beautiful and thin as they are there are only thirty-five minutes left for news. And if you take away the time the weather and sports are on there is not much time left for news

stories. So to get the smorgasbord of information, the servings must be compact. One minute and thirty seconds compact, like eating sushi—small but tasty and full of nutrition.

Please don't complain to the CRTC about this. In America the average length of a news story is down to about one minute and ten seconds, so we are much smarter.

Anyway, if the stories go over a minute thirty here there are fewer stories, and that means fewer fascinating facts about new crimes, new politicians, new trends, new problems, new solutions to old problems and new discoveries on what we should not eat, late breaking fires, scandals, floods, earthquakes, traffic jams and more weather. Hence 1:30 is a good rule.

And to get things into that time you have to leave out other things without leaving out the important things. That is the impossible job of the editor.

Greg saw all the beautiful pictures of the castle. That was what the story was about. Listening to Shirley talk about building it was also what the story was about.

In the allotted time it was done. One minute and thirty seconds, exactly. Perfect—but no Marilyn. She didn't make the cut.

"We have to get her in," I said. "Can you imagine the two of them watching tonight and only one is on the screen?"

Greg smiled his understanding smile. "Not good."

All Marilyn did was join us on the porch for a minute. She didn't build the castle, but every bit as important as the majestic dwelling was the majestic twosome who lived in the old wooden house with the castle in the window.

In short, she had to be there or we would be cheating the fact that they both lived there. It is not a stretch. This is what goes into a brief story about an aluminum foil castle built for Christmas.

He trimmed a bit of this and a bit of that. He chipped away at one picture of a turret that seemed too long anyway, and in the end Marilyn joined us on the porch for a few moments.

Nice.

When I got home after the show I got an email from an old friend. He wanted to know how we had found the women and then said that very recently his daughter had told him and her mother that she was gay.

All he wanted for her was happiness. All he wanted was that she not have to hide, and what he saw in the story was two women living together who seemed happy and not hiding. It made him feel good. It made his daughter feel good. They didn't have to say anything.

And in truth, we have no idea what Shirley and Marilyn's relationship is, and it is none of our business. We should not even be thinking about it, but they were happy, and both of them were in the story—and the castle was not the only place that housed royalty.

Dancing, with Women

I have this friend named Grant Faint. I see him once every five years, sometimes less, but I see his work every day. He is one of the world's leading photographers and I do not exaggerate.

Many of the advertisements you see for beer or perfume or aquariums with whales on one side of the glass and a little girl on the other are his.

You don't call him brilliant; that underplays his talent. You don't call him rich; that underplays his worth.

He started out poor—dirt poor, if that is still a phrase. He told me that at Christmas the church people came and put food in his parents' refrigerator. If they hadn't, it would have been empty.

He came from the East Side of Vancouver when that meant you had no money. He shot a television news camera for years, always, and I mean always, getting pictures that no one else did. He was closest to the fires, he was there at the scene of the crime, he got the tears in the reunions.

Then he quit. He could not stand working with reporters who

asked stupid questions. In fact if he thought the reporter was asking too many questions during interviews he would unplug the cable from the camera to the microphone and go off taking pictures of the event they were covering.

The poor reporter, either too new or too self-centred, who did not know how to ask questions in the first place would go on asking questions unaware that the cable to his microphone was lying on the ground. And if the subject of the interview was a politician then that subject would keep on talking. It's a reflex—see microphone, open mouth.

If you were to try that now you would be up in front of the human resources department. They would be telling you how you were undermining the integrity and reputation of another employee, which is not tolerated, and there would be no further warnings.

The difference with the reporters Grant worked with was they learned how to ask better, shorter questions.

Anyway, after he quit he took a great many pictures and sent them to a company that sold stock photos to advertising agencies. He sent them many, many pictures. Eventually an agency bought one. Then they bought more. Now his photos constitute a significant portion of the company's inventory.

He spends much of the year travelling and taking pictures. In short, he has been everywhere and seen everything. With some of his profits he has built an orphanage and a medical clinic in Africa.

He is a good guy.

He sent me a note yesterday. He was in a small town in China. It ended with:

> ps last night i was in a town square about 40 people dancing outside in dark old style ballroom dancing older folks ...
> so that is not new BUT there was this couple one was a very old lady clinging onto her dance partner
> she could move only a bit her dance partner her daughter who was maybe 60 herself the two of them

totally in love just sharing a moment together mother and her child dancing in the dark both with lovely smiling faces enjoying a

simple life together soon the mother will pass and the memory will be in my head and yours

grant.

He did not send a picture, but you can see it. Just close your eyes—a story that is now in my head and yours.

Thank you.

The Tree and the Carver

First of all, I do not like doing stories about Native carvers. There are so many of them and so many are so good and many of them have the same story:

"I had a hard life and turned to carving."

That is true. They did have hard times, often brought upon themselves, like many, many of the rest of us. One good thing for some Native carvers is they have something they could hold, a piece of wood or stone. It is good to hold something when you also have a tradition that a Great Spirit made that wood or stone.

Yes, you still need talent, or at least massive perseverance, and you still have to learn from someone else and you still have to be sober and you still have to sell the thing after you have carved it. Ask any artist or writer or inventor or person with a resume: selling what you have is usually the hardest part. It is when most who have done everything else give up.

Pass the carvers sitting by the side of the street and look. You don't have to understand art. You can see that is a beautiful eagle or bear. And it is made of stone or wood. And the artist is right there in front of you. You could ask him about his work.

Go ahead, buy a piece and you will be happy. You'll even have a story that goes with it, and that you get for free.

But it is hard for me to do stories about them simply because there are so many of them. "You did a story about him; what about me?"

But sometimes there are exceptions.

As always, we were looking for something. There was a man in a wheelchair looking out at the ocean, a sad but beautiful sight. We stopped and I could hear him yelling profanities, which was not so beautiful. He went on his way, still yelling, and I looked out at the sea and back and forth, and there, just over the Seawall and almost hidden, was a fellow sitting on a stool. Looking more closely I could see he was a carver, but there was something very different about him. It wasn't so much his art as where he was doing it.

In front of him was a little maple tree, behind him the rocks of the Seawall, and between the two were about two steps of sand. Okay, I think, this is his studio. And that was all I was thinking when I leaned over the rock wall and spoke to him.

"Nice little spot you have," I said. You have to start somewhere.

He nodded.

"Been here long?"

He nodded.

"High tide," I said.

He looked up at me. "King tide," he said.

Super-high tide. The water was not far from his toes. What a beautiful picture—an artist's studio with no room for him to move his feet. That was the kind of stuff a Hollywood film starts with.

"Hi, we're from CTV. Can we talk to you?"

"Who are you?"

I love that; someone who is pure and not part of television and is not interested in someone who makes a living from it.

I told him. He shrugged. I was happy.

Jock was his name and he said he had worked in the corporate world but had been pushed out of it. That happens. The only thing that hurts more is when those doing the firing tell you, "This hurts me more than you can imagine."

To mend his soul Jock had walked around Vancouver's path by the ocean, which is better than going to a therapist or psychiatrist, or taking pills or drugs or drinking. Try it. It works.

He passed a spit of land that had the broken branches of a sapling sticking out of the sand. They barely came up to his knees. He was told that the Park Board had ordered it to be cut down, and each time it grew back they cut it down again. This happened three times.

"It was broken, like me," he said.

He climbed over the Seawall and decided that was the spot where he would look for his own rebirth. It was also where he could protect something besides himself. That was ten years ago.

Every day he walked to the broken tree, climbed down from the Seawall and set up his stool and his pieces of stone, and there he spent the day cutting, carving, sanding and turning stone into art.

By the time we met him the tree was twice his height. If the Park Board workers had come by during the day they would not have touched it. There is a policy against confrontations—and the gardeners don't work at night.

"It is my living room," he said.

The way he said "living" he did not mean it was like a room in a house. He meant it was his place for living.

"The tree has grown strong, and I have too."

I went away feeling good—and worried. Long ago I met two women who put socks and cookies in plastic baggies and hung them from a small Christmas-looking tree in one of the parking lots of Stanley Park.

The Park Board took down the baggies. The women put them

back. The Park Board took them down, the women replaced them. Down, up, down, up.

"You just can't change the natural surroundings like that," was the official position.

Then the women hung more baggies with socks on the tree, decorating it just like a Christmas tree should be decorated.

Finally those in charge of everything could stand it no more and they cut down the tree.

"We have a policy, and you know that," were the official words of the official response. "What if everyone did that, what then?"

The tree Jock is looking after is growing on the wrong side of the Seawall. That is why they cut it down.

I fear someday Jock will show up and his tree will be gone. If it happens I will let you know, but meanwhile go by and visit. Look at his tree and his art and his living room. It is right down from the Sylvia Hotel. You will feel good.

Close My Eyes

Some stories are little more than an image. I close my eyes and I see a bride in white, in a wedding gown, and her husband in a tux, all black of course.

They are standing in the rain. No, not just rain—pouring, drenching rain. They are standing in front of the lighthouse at Brockton Point in Stanley Park. Someone, a friend, is taking their picture.

"Why?"

"We came up here a few years ago from California. He asked me to marry him right here," she said.

They went back to California, lived, worked, got married, and then she said, "I want a wedding picture by the lighthouse."

What about the rain?

"What could be better?" she said. "I won't remember the other pictures."

Brockton Point Lighthouse is much more than just a beautiful backdrop. It was extremely important for all the years before radar, keeping wooden ships from sinking, which many sailors were happy about.

One of the duties of the lighthouse keeper in the 1800s and early 1900s was to tell the fishermen it was time to come home for supper.

You just might know about this because it was in an earlier book, *Haunting Vancouver*, a good book if I say so myself, but if you missed it I'll tell you again.

And the neat thing about telling you this is that it is basic to my philosophy on collecting stories that might be worth telling. Every time I go by the lighthouse with someone who doesn't know the story I say, "Do you know what the old lighthouse keeper did when he wasn't lighthouse keeping?"

"No," they say.

"Ahhh," I say, and then I tell them this story:

A century and a half ago the fishermen, mostly looking for salmon, were in small boats, really just large rowboats. Before dawn they would row out into Burrard Inlet or further out past the first narrows.

They would use rod and line, hook and bait, and try to catch salmon, one at a time. They would be there all day. They brought some food—often dried salmon—for lunch, and some beer and bread, and they pulled in one fish after another. If they stopped to rest they were not making any money.

If it rained they got wet. Most of them had a small pup tent in the middle of the boat, but that was only for when it was really coming down, as it was on the wedding couple. Even on those days they still held their rods out from inside the tent.

Their day was supposed to end at six o'clock but they didn't have watches or clocks (can you imagine a watch in a rowboat filled with fish and water?) so what to do? That is where the lighthouse keeper came in.

At the top of the hour he would tie a stick of dynamite onto the

59

end of a fishing line, pick up the pole, light the fuse and cast the explosive out as far as he could—even farther if the adrenalin kicked in.

Bang! Or rather *BANG!*

"I thought it would never come," said the fishermen, and they rowed back in and sold their fish to the middlemen who took them to the canneries, which helped build what was at one time British Columbia's second-biggest industry.

Then came a gift from Victoria. It was not really a heartfelt gift. The keepers of the capital were just trying to clean out their closets, and over there, taking up valuable space where they could put a statue of a politician, was an old cannon.

"What shall we do with it?"

"Give it to Vancouver. They'll take anything," one may or may not have said.

So they shipped it over the strait and the Vancouver aldermen said, "Wonderful. But what shall we do with it?"

The new Stanley Park was desperate for any kind of decoration, so there it went—a decoration and a possible lifesaver. Can you imagine what would have happened if the line had got tangled while the lighthouse keeper was casting out the sizzling dynamite?

So with city officials standing around the cannon, six o'clock came and a half-pound of gunpowder was ignited.

BOOM!! That was a really big *BOOM!!* Much bigger than the *BANG!* of the dynamite.

It was basically the biggest, loudest dinner bell in the country, maybe the world, and at six o'clock every night for a while the Six o'Clock Gun was fired. Yes, it was called the Six o'Clock Gun. What else would you call it?

That is, until the mothers who were trying to get their kids to eat dinner could take it no longer.

The boom was heard loud and clear across the city. It shook windowpanes and dishes and the concentration of little ones eating their burgers and fries. Okay, there were no burgers and fries then, but no doubt the kids were dreaming of them.

"Stop running to the window," said the mothers to their misbehaving children.

The next night it happened again: *BOOM!!* And the next: *BOOM!!*

Finally some of the women of Vancouver marched on City Hall and demanded a stop to the gun play.

"But we are not playing," the city fathers might or might not have told them. "This is serious manly business. We are telling the time."

The mothers might or might not have said, "Well stop or we'll give you a miserable time all the time."

If you are married you know that's a convincing argument. The fishermen were not consulted, but the politicians had to make a hard decision, they said. Politicians are always saying that, as though the rest of us don't.

Anyhow, the politicians decided in favour of the women in front of them rather than the fishermen who were way out in the dark on the water waiting to be called in to eat.

In a short time the booms were changed to nine p.m. and the gun then became the . . . well, you know.

That is what I think of when I close my eyes and conjure up an image of the Brockton Point Lighthouse.

And what I always say (I know I'm boring about it) is get a story you can tell, and tell it. It beats television.

Some of the stories that come to mind are not really stories. They don't have the beginning, middle and end that all stories need, but some of them are still memorable.

I was near Sunset Beach when a woman pedalled past me on her bike. Then she stopped and came back.

Her name was Beatrice and I had bought airplane tickets from her a long time ago, before everyone did everything on computers. That was when we talked to each other.

She reminded me of meeting her and then said out of the blue, "The story I liked most was the little girl from Germany who was making dandelion bracelets for herself."

That was at least thirty-five years ago.

"I loved that one too," I said, and truly I did.

There was something so simple and beautiful about a girl, maybe ten or twelve years old, in a park near downtown passing the time and making art that would last such a short time.

I remember her saying her father was in a conference and that he travelled around the world and often brought her with him. She had nothing else to do while she waited for him.

There were no other adults around, which I then did not find unusual. Now I wouldn't dare speak to a kid without a parent nearby and without asking the parent for permission.

In fact now, as you know, you would find very few ten- or twelve-year-olds, especially girls, out by themselves.

The world has changed. It is turned upside down from the way kids were two generations ago. Now the parks are mostly empty, unless there are adults watching the kids. The streets have fewer and fewer hockey games abuzz with shouting ten-year-olds.

Of course there are still some, but a few decades ago all the streets were filled with them. Now there is fear of being outside combined with video games that keep you inside and texting and earbuds that keep out all sounds of living except for the programmed hit music.

Street hockey? Not today. It's sad.

The scene of the girl making the bracelets from yellow flowers was beautiful. It made Beatrice and me feel good to remember it— and nothing happened in that story. Maybe that's the story.

High-Class Dining

Today is Family Day. I have a cold. I have the flu. I am dying. This will be a challenge. My head hurts, my chest hurts . . . I could go on but you had the same flu sometime over the winter so you know what hurts. We might have given it to each other.

Yes, I could stay home, but everything would hurt just as much and there would be no chance of getting the pain out of my mind. At least if I am working I may think of something else and I will feel less awful.

No, I will not infect anyone now. I am told the infection period was two weeks ago when I didn't know I had the illness and I might have said hello to you. Sorry. That proves bacteria are very smart. They know how to get around before they are discovered. Bacteria evolved long before us.

I am trying Reilly's method. "I am not sick. I *really* am not sick. *Darn* it, I really, really am *not* sick."

Oh, golly. I am so sick.

It is a clear sky so I don't need to look for a hole in the clouds, and anyway it hurts just to look up, but I need help.

We stop at Sunset Beach. A family—mother, daughter, son and baby carriage—are going for hot chocolate. Father is working.

"Can we take a picture?"

Yes.

There's a start.

A fine big fellow is putting out plastic chairs around the metal tables, and I have an idea.

This is not a hot dog stand. No. This is a four-star restaurant for which you need reservations. So in the story for television I say that, while four-year-old Simon climbs onto one of the plastic chairs.

His sister, Adaline, puts on her coat. "It's cold," she says.

She is dressing for dinner, I say.

Their mother, Carmen, brings the hot chocolate. It is a Michelin Two Star creation, I say, with whipped cream on top.

Adaline and Simon begin licking the sweet, thickened white mountain on top of the chocolate. In this super-polite society at this fancy restaurant that is the only way to eat whipped cream.

And then, after Carmen lifts the baby from the carriage, Simon spontaneously gets out of his chair followed by Adaline and they hug their little brother along with their mother.

It's a tangle of arms and faces, all cozy and safe. That warm, nourishing entrée is served only in the best places and to the best families.

I'm feeling much better, and I've done nothing.

How Does It Happen?

How does it consistently happen? I ask this over and over and it still happens over and over. It has done so for decades and it still leaves me dumbfounded.

And my point is that it could happen to you. You could have an adventure every day or whenever you want it. You don't need to do this for a living. You can do it just for living.

You don't need a TV station or newspaper behind you. You don't need an audience other than the person sitting across the table where your teriyaki chicken is waiting, or if you are vegetarian then you can talk about this over carrots. Everything works.

You just look for something neat or offbeat or colourful or weird or funny or sad (not a lot of that, because there is already too much) and tell the person you are eating with what you found. Simple.

Don't worry about how you will tell it. It will come out fine. You don't need to be a writer to tell a story, you just need the story. It can be one sentence or it can last the whole meal.

I tell many people this. It is better than collecting stamps. If you are young, stamps are things that you put on an envelope before mailing it.

Sorry. An envelope is a folded piece of paper in which you put a letter.

Sorry again. A letter is a piece of paper on which you write something with a pen, and a pen . . . oh forget it.

What I am talking about is better than collecting money. Now there is a stretch of reality, right?

Money, of course, will make you rich, but then the Canadian dollar will fall and you will be poor or the stock market will dive and that will have the same result. You will get sick and worry yourself to death, so forget about that.

Stories are gold. Gold is not bad in itself but stories are better. The more you share them the richer you are, and that's not true of the gold coins that you have hidden somewhere in a jar in . . . well, somewhere, but you can't tell where because, well, you know. Just *don't worry* about them. No one will take them. *Don't worry!*

See? Stories are better.

"Where should we go?" Todd Gilchrist asked.

"Left, then right, then left, then straight. Or go somewhere else."

We had a goal, not a destination. We wanted to find something nice, happy—you know the rest.

We make a loop downtown and there is nothing. It starts to rain, which means that less than nothing is waiting for us. Whoever was out before, which was no one, has gone back inside where sensible people go when it is raining, and whoever was inside is not coming out.

"Maybe Queen Elizabeth Park," I say.

"You're only saying that because we're at 33rd and Main and the park is just over there," says Todd.

"Over there" is one block away, and soon we're at the park.

"I haven't been here for years," he says.

Why not? I think, but I don't say it because there is no point in questioning someone who has my daily salary in his hands.

If he doesn't take good pictures I can't do a story and if I can't do that there is no pay. So I won't question his lack of going places that I think are worth going. Don't do it.

"So why don't you come here?" I ask.

"Too far."

Okay, that's a good answer.

"But you are missing the conservatory," I say, "which has birds and fish and trees and neat stuff."

"I played volleyball with my wife last night," he said.

Okay again. Volleyball with his wife is better than birds and fish and trees.

"Did you know this is a reservoir?" I said, pointing down at the parking lot.

"Nope, didn't know that," he said.

"Did you know the whole park was once a volcano?" I said. (I'll tell you later how I learned that.)

"Nope, didn't know that either," he said with the same enthusiasm.

So I tried something that would work on someone who lives in today's world: "Did you know there used to be a lot of drug deals up here?"

"Really?"

"Yep, I used to come up here looking to find someone bird watching, except the bird watchers were scared away. You can't bring binoculars to a place where ugly-looking guys are passing packages back and forth," I said.

I told him you could watch a car pull into the lot, circle once or twice and then pull up alongside a parked car. The window went down on the passenger side of one car, then the window on the driver's side of the other car went down.

One arm went out with something and dropped it in the other car. Then an arm came out from the other car and dropped something in the first car. Then both cars left.

Imagine this happening right next to the glass dome with the birds and fish living in a garden of warmth and peace and love.

"No drug dealers now," Todd said.

"Nope." I pointed at the southwest corner of the lot where there is a giant antenna with spikes and hoops sticking up about four storeys.

"The police put one of their transmission relays here. The drug dealers were sure it was heavy with cameras, which it probably is, and presto, puff. Drug dealers gone."

"Neat," said Todd.

But no story, and the rain was coming harder.

We saw someone with a red shirt and cowboy hat playing golf on the pitch and putt course. Todd grabbed his camera and jumped out.

That is good, except the red shirt is way over there and we are way over here. We watched him hit a ball and run after it, then hit it again and run again.

"He's running faster than us," I said. "And it's in the other direction."

Todd got back in his suv.

"Where should we go?" Todd asked.

"Kingsway," I said.

Someone at work had sent me a note about seeing a man dancing with a sign in front of a used furniture store. It is hard getting a note like this because I don't want to tell him that many people have that dancing job.

The difference between me and the fellow who sent me the note is he had never seen it before. He was excited. He wanted to share it, and that is exactly what I tell everyone they should do.

Go out every day and actively look for something, anything, and when you find it tell someone. I tell people that is what I do every day and I am lucky to have made a career out of it.

But what happens when someone tells you something that you already know about?

You could say, "Oh, yeah, you think a pink-spotted parrot is something? I've seen pink-spotted parrots all over town."

"Yeah, well, the one I saw had a lot of spots."

"How many?"

"How do I know how many? I didn't count but it had a lot and I don't believe that you've seen any pink-spotted parrots."

"Oh, yeah, you want to fight?"

And that is the way wars start.

In my case, I just did not want to disappoint the fellow who had told me about the dancing man with the sign.

"Kingsway," I said. "There's a fellow dancing with a sign."

"Seen many of them," said Todd.

"Maybe this one will be different. Maybe this one will have prosthetic legs and will be an inspiration. Maybe."

I pause for a reality check.

"Well, at least he'll be dancing in the rain and that's something, sort of."

We get to the used furniture store. No one is dancing. No one is walking. No one is standing. Everyone is smart. It is raining.

"Okay. Trout Lake," I said.

Trout Lake you will read about many times. Properly called John Hendry Park, it is at Victoria Drive and 15th Avenue, and it is the motherlode of all golden stories. If you haven't been there, do go and visit.

It has a pond surrounded by a walking path. At one end is a dog park where your unleashed friends can swim. At the other end is the smallest beach in the city, with sand and a lifeguard.

You can walk around the pond from the beach to the dogs in five minutes, without speeding.

In the late 1800s and early 1900s it supplied fresh water for the giant Hastings Sawmill (owned by John Hendry) on Burrard Inlet where Vancouver was actually born. I once found part of a wooden pipe that carried the water that long, long distance. The pipe was at the north end, just where a couple of dogs were splashing in the water.

A few months later I tried to show someone where it was, but nature had taken it back and I never saw the pipe again.

But the best part of the park is the people. Victoria Drive was originally inhabited by folks who worked on the railroad or in sawmills or corner grocery stores and they all walked to work.

Their kids grew up with the pond as their world. They were lucky kids. The parents could let them play there all day without worry. Lucky parents.

Now, no more railroad, no sawmills, and the corner stores are either turned into homes or coffee shops and no one walks to work.

But they are the same people. It's their neighbourhood, their park, and if you go there you will feel like it is your park.

Unlike Stanley or Queen Elizabeth Parks, there are no tourists and no one is parking their luxury car in the lot. Also, unlike those parks, the parking at Trout Lake is free. Okay, read that line again. It's true.

There are no statues of people who were never in the park. There is only one painting of one woman, and I will tell you about her later. There is no army of gardeners (just one who is super) and there are no sculptures of things that you are not sure what those things are, but there are baseball fields, which are used. The big parks don't have baseball.

I once saw a Little League game being played there—a lot of shouting and cheering and pinging of balls against aluminum bats, all the things that make baseball good—and then I saw something better.

Outside the wire-caged dugout was one boy, maybe twelve, who was throwing a ball into a glove on his hand. It was hypnotic. It was beautiful. If you play baseball you know that many good hours have been spent just throwing a ball into a glove. It feels good.

"What you doing?" I asked, knowing he was going to say,

"Nothing," because throwing a ball into a glove is nothing when you have to explain it.

But no. This kid said, "I'm breaking in a glove."

Well, that's nice. In fact that's a painstaking art that takes a long time.

"It's my coach's glove."

Now it is beautiful.

"Why?"

"My team's not playing today and I came down here to watch and he asked me to."

It was like the girl making a bracelet out of dandelions. Breaking in a glove, making something from flowers, both doing nothing if you asked them, and yet both doing something on a level of transcendental meditation, whatever that means, or even better.

So I was thinking of those things when I said, "Let's try Trout Lake."

But before we could set off there came a sign from on high, and you can't ignore that. This one was on the second floor of a building on Kingsway. It said "Billiards" and it had Chinese writing around it.

Perfect. Indoors. No rain. Two old guys playing for years and neither one better than the other.

As Todd and I walked to the front door we passed a brake and muffler shop on the other side of the parking lot.

"No matter how bad this is," I said, "it's better than working over there."

Todd nodded.

My imagination was pumping as we approached the pool hall.

Two guys are up there. They don't speak English, so I don't have to interview them, but someone in the pool hall knows them and tells us their history.

They grew up together, moved here together, worked together, maybe even both became widowers about the same time. The more I thought about it the better it became.

One problem: the door was locked. Someone passed by and said they open only at night.

That was disappointing. Of course we would go on to Trout Lake, but now the camera, which had come out of the truck again, was going back in. Another defeat, and defeats may make the spirit stronger but they are not good in real life.

While Todd was locking in the camera (it is not good to go to the boss and say someone took it) I looked across the parking lot at the brake shop. Above the noise of the traffic on Kingsway, I could hear music—not the chest-vibrating mega-pulsing of hard rock like I would expect from a brake shop, but something that was almost opera.

I walked closer. It was in another language and it was sweet and smooth and calming.

A worker walked up to me.

"Nice music," I said.

"Vietnamese," he said.

"Oh," I said, brilliantly. "Why?"

"We are Vietnamese," he said.

"Who?"

"We. He and me," he said pointing to another mechanic.

"Does your boss like the music?"

"We are the bosses."

"Oh," I said again, this time like I had just won the lottery, because at that moment the sun came out, flowers were blooming and if there had been a choir nearby they would have been singing.

Of course it was still raining and cold and miserable, but if they are the bosses then there is a story here that needs telling.

I told him who we were and what we would like and he said, "Oh, no. I don't want to be on television."

I think, Oh yes, you do.

"Just show us the music," I say.

"No," he says.

I can see he will need some coaxing or I will need some cyanide pills for myself.

"Just show us the records," I start to say, and then change it to "CDs," which I think is up to date.

He looks at me in a strange way.

"Show us how you play it," I say and somehow out of pity he leads us to the back of the shop where there is a small box under large speakers.

He picks up a tiny thing and even though most of you know what it is, I don't. But he has on white rubber gloves with grease stains on them and I know Todd is pointing his camera at his hands and I am happy.

Honestly, to me it is like a moment with Picasso. It is little things that make everything good, and right now it is a neat, clean computer thing held by hands in greasy work gloves.

He pushes something and out comes beautiful music. It is not rock, it is sweet and smooth and a woman's voice.

"What is she saying?" I ask.

"She's singing a poem about the night coming and everything will be all right."

He looks happy telling me.

"What else do you like about it?" I ask.

And that is when he started telling us that it reminded him of his childhood and his parents and what the moon looked like when he was little and the excitement of everything.

In short I was listening to a monologue of memories while the song played softly behind him. Todd was recording it and that alone was good enough to tell the world.

For a fellow who did not want to talk he would not stop. Then he introduced us to his partner. The third owner was away on vacation in Vietnam.

"How did you wind up here?" I asked.

"I was born in a refugee camp in Malaysia," said the second fellow.

"I was one of the boat people," said the first guy.

They had worked for someone else who had owned the shop for several years until he quit and sold it to them.

"Now we work twice as hard, but it is ours," said the one born in a camp.

I was warm and happy. A couple of hard-working fellows who started with nothing and now have something and they keep their history alive with music.

Then one changed the music and out came rap.

"Vietnamese rap," he said. "Don't know how that got in there."

And I am thinking, what could be better.

And we were done.

And, as I asked a bunch of pages ago, how does it happen? I have no idea.

Trout Lake

*A*fter leaving the brake and muffler shop we passed Trout Lake, with all the memories and stories that it holds for me, all from one park:

Mona, who drives every day when the weather is good from New Westminster to a park bench near the lake to have her lunch, is a sweetheart. Her skin is wrinkled. "I'm eighty-nine for God's sake. Of course my skin is wrinkled—but give me a hug."

Yes, I can't wait.

The first time I met her I asked to look in her lunch bag. How else can you get to know someone? In addition to a sandwich and thermos she had a can of WD-40, a wrench and a set of screwdrivers.

"Why?"

"Well suppose someone needed something and I didn't have it. What then?"

I knew at that moment I was in love.

The first story I did about her was simply her daily trip.

"Why?"

"I like it here," she said.

I wrote about her several books ago.

She was born nearby, she grew up swimming in the lake and getting in trouble with her mother because she would go home covered with mud. She met her husband near the park. She got married near the park. She raised a family here.

"What more reasons would anyone have?" she asked.

"But it is a long drive."

"Only if you think it is," she said with deep wisdom. Time and space is not what we think it is—or it is whatever anyone thinks it is. It's a short drive if you want it to be. That was good enough for one story.

The second came about when a friend of Mona's was chatting with her when we arrived.

"Want to know the real reason she comes here?" said the friend.

Mona raised her fist from the seat at the picnic table.

"Don't you dare tell," she said, but it was half a laugh, like one of those things you want someone to tell but you have to protest.

"Please tell," I said.

"She buried her husband's ashes under this table," the friend said.

Mona was beaming, embarrassed, beautiful. She smiled. She was mischievous. She was a law breaker. You can't spread ashes anywhere in public spaces, but she was in love. She was married fifty years.

"I told you not to tell," she said to her friend.

"She also sprinkled some in the lake," he said.

"Oh, come on. Now no one will swim in there," said Mona.

This is in a lake that has been around at least a thousand years, now with constant aeration from a tall pipe that sucks up the water and shoots it out ten feet above the surface, with dogs swimming at one end and kids at the other. As I said, it even has a lifeguard.

"No one cares," said Mona's friend.

Now we know why she makes the trip.

And there is one other thing you should see if you go there to visit her. About fifty steps from her bench is a steel storage shed.

The gardener keeps his tools inside. In a rare good move by the Park Board they hired someone to paint flowers and trees on the shed. He got some neighbourhood kids to help.

He was painting when we were talking to Mona. He listened to the conversation and then went back to work.

By the time Mona had finished her lunch and was heading back to her volunteer work at the food bank in New West, he had painted a picture of her sitting at her table eating her lunch.

If you pass by someday and see the shed, you'll know why there is a picture of a woman with snow-white hair in the park—the only one.

The picture will be there for a long time. I hope Mona is too.

Then there was the little lost pony. There was a picture posted on a wooden pole, saying "LOST." It's good to check everything that you pass by. You never know what prizes may be there.

"LOST. One plastic pony, three inches high. Brown. Reward." There was a phone number. We called.

Yes, a small boy had lost his favourite toy in the park.

"Did you find it?" his mother asked.

"Sorry, no. But would you like us to help?"

Helping is always nice. We did a story with the boy describing his pony and the next day, presto, a woman called the boy. She had found it.

Story number two about the pony: the reward was five dollars, but the finder turned it down. When the boy insisted that she take it she did, and then she walked with him and his mother and the pony around the corner where they got ice cream.

I looked out over the grass in the park. There is a lot of it, but somehow the woman had happened to be looking down at the exact moment that she was passing over the lost pony.

She hadn't seen the poster. She didn't know someone was looking for it but, instead of just passing over it when she realized it was just a tiny, lost toy, she picked it up. She thought there was no chance on earth that she would ever find the owner but she held onto it just in case.

Then she watched the news.

The first story ended with the boy almost crying. The second story ended with him eating ice cream and trying to feed some to his pony.

It's a pity every story can't end like that.

Locked Out

When I first saw her I said we will talk to anyone but her.

The girl was sitting in the pagoda in the middle of the park. It is really just a place to get out of the rain. It has several picnic tables and benches.

Her head was down on a table. She has problems, I thought.

I walked by her, just to see if she was crying or showed any sign of needing help but all I could see were her hands cupping her head and her face pointed down.

Not good. I would not step into her world.

Instead we wandered the park. We wandered here and there and back to here. There is no point in detailing each failure. We all have them and if we talk about them too much it gets tiresome.

But we found nothing. A *big* failure here today. Okay, I admit that sometimes Trout Lake, the jewel of parks, lets me down. On the other hand, maybe it's not the fault of the park. Maybe it's mine.

That's possible. That hurts, but perhaps I haven't looked

somewhere for something and have given up too soon. Don't we all do that?

I looked back at the girl. She was sitting in the same spot. You never know. I took a long walk back to the pagoda.

This will be bad but at least I'll try, I thought. She will have problems with her boyfriend, her family, her teachers, her life, everything. I will regret this.

"Excuse me, it's none of my business, but are you okay?"

She could have told me that I was right, it was none of my business, but no, this girl just spoke up and ruined the whole idea that the park could let me down.

"I'm locked out of my house and this is the best place to wait."

What? Locked out of her house? A universal experience! Oh beauty, oh joy. The poor girl is locked out. We've all been there. Everyone at one time or another has stuck their hands in their pockets and said, "Uh oh. Where are they? Oh no!" She was one of us.

I told you the park was good.

She had left her keys at home when she went to school. Now she had to wait for her mother or her brother, she said.

"I sure hope it's my mother who comes home first."

"Why?"

"Because last time my brother forgot his keys I kept him sitting out on the porch for twenty minutes before I let him in. He'll do the same to me."

Bless you, and your problem. On television you were so sweet and you made everyone who has done the same thing remember that time.

I told you the park was good, and I almost missed it because I was afraid of talking to someone who looked like she had a problem.

That would have made me the one with the problem.

In all, I have done more than one hundred stories at Trout Lake. On the other hand I have done more than one thousand stories in Stanley Park. Yes, that's true. Someone at a previous television station once counted them. She stopped at a thousand.

Now it's your turn. Queen Elizabeth Park is good too, but just go to your local park. They are all places with people who have lives outside of television and work, like you. There is always potential for you to find something interesting there. Go on, find something and enjoy.

Beyond Belief

"Stop. She's got goldfish in her shoes!"

Right there, right on the diamond-studded golden concrete of Robson Street (of course it's not really diamonds and gold but you have to have diamonds and gold to afford to shop on that street), right there was a woman walking with her fish.

This is cruel. This is stupid. This is the kind of story that doesn't need a beginning, middle or end. The sheer idiocy is enough to support it.

She was wearing shoes with plastic cube-like heels filled with water and in the water in her heels were goldfish, two in each one.

"Are they real?" I asked.

Of course I could see they were real. She meant for all to see that they were real.

"Aren't they cute?" she said.

I couldn't answer. It was inhumane, it was thoughtless, it was mean, but I didn't want to sound like a confrontational do-gooder, so I just said, "You think they are going to live?"

"I had to take them back yesterday because they were dead," she said. "They sold me bad fish."

It's not the fish who are bad, I thought.

"Why?" I asked.

"I told you, because they were dead."

"No, I mean why are you wearing that? Them?"

She tilted her head, trying to make sense of the question.

"It's stylish," she said. "Everyone will have them soon."

Meanwhile video of the fish and the heels and the shoes was being gathered, and her words were being collected and my sympathy for the fish was building steam.

"You know they bounce around in there and that can kill them."

Her head tilted the other way.

"I wouldn't hurt them for the world. And there's even a way I can twist open the heels and free them," she said with care and kindness and even sincerity in her voice.

I looked down. "I think you have another dead one."

She looked down. She could see one of them floating upside down, which had happened just since we'd started talking.

She was angry.

"That does it. They sold me another sick fish. I'll take them back right now and get my money back."

"Do you have another pair of shoes to wear?"

"I'll buy some," she said. "After I give them a piece of my mind."

And then she left, beating to death the three terrified remaining fish with each step she took back to the store, where she would complain—about the fish.

A piece of her mind she would give them, she said. That wouldn't leave her with much.

The Painted House

Stephen Harper, the politician who would not tolerate any deviation from his way of thinking in his people, was in Richmond.

He was promoting a new program that would help families and help him get re-elected.

What he needed was a typical immigrant family with children. He would stand in front of their home and make the announcement.

Early in the morning painters arrived at the home. They painted the front as high as they could reach, but no higher. No ladders, just tiptoes.

They did not paint the sides of the house, which could have used some paint.

Also early in the morning his people (isn't it great to have people?) went to a toy store where they bought a great selection of really great large toys.

They spread them around the yard in a way that would make a parent furious at kids who would leave their toys out like that. Yes, this is plain fraud. This is deception. This is the way political leaders work even with kids and toys.

Then his people used yellow tape to mark off the place where the television cameras would be allowed. From that position they could see only the front of the house and only if they pointed up, away from where the prime minister would be speaking, would they see the unpainted part. And they would not do that because they were paid to record his speech.

As he left the house to stand in front of the cameras he passed by the toys. The cameras always follow him as he walks to the podium.

It was an image of love and family and fun and gay abandon and children and peace and happiness. Of course, it was a lie.

And then he spoke of whatever it was he was speaking of and left immediately by limousine for his next speech.

The cameras left, following him.

His people gathered up the toys and drove back to the toy store where they returned everything for a full refund.

And the rest of the house remained unpainted.

But on television, where the prime minister stood in front of a bright and clean house surrounded by the objects of joy and happiness, it all looked so real, as did the man giving the speech.

A Real Garden

We went to the Northwest Flower & Garden Show in Seattle. It is one of the largest and most beautiful anywhere.

The normal thing for a reporter to say here is, it is the second-largest in the US or it is one of the ten largest in the world. And then you get to thinking is it really so?

Then you go to Google and do some instant researching, and that's followed by converting the US square feet into international metric and then you have to decide whether to include the sellers of seeds and garden gloves in the show or just stick with the actual gardens.

Sometimes reporters should be outlawed from reporting.

So my wife and I were walking around the show, and the gardens were utterly beautiful. One had a volcano with smoke drifting up and up and up. It was probably fifteen feet tall, or whatever that is in metric.

"That would be nice," my wife said.

I thought about how we could get a volcano in our front yard and what the passing dogs would think—or do.

And there was a woodland scene with a fallen tree and a stream and ferns and rocks and leaves. It was so real I thought I was anywhere in Lynn Valley.

There was a desert land scrapping. I know that's not a word, but "landscape" is boring. It's a label. Land scrapping is active and that is what this was, with cactus and dried rocks and sand. I thought an old prospector with his mule would soon walk out of it.

But in none of the gardens was there any place to sit and drink beer—or vitamin-infused natural spring water—while enjoying a quiet afternoon after working yourself to exhaustion making your garden look natural. These were not real gardens. These were works of art.

There were no lawn mowers or empty bags of soil enhancers that you'd brought home from the supermarket along with eggs and milk. That was when the bags of soil were full and heavy and it was raining and some of it spilled over your coat and then the bags leaked in the trunk.

That's what makes a real garden. Those in Seattle lacked the human element, but they were beautiful and inspiring.

"We should go home and do something," my wife said.

She is beautiful and I was inspired.

By the time we got home it was dark and raining. When she opened the car door it got caught in the foot-high fence that lines the driveway. It is there to look pretty.

When she closed the door it ripped up the fence.

"I'm sorry," I said. "I parked too close."

"I'll fix it in the morning," she said.

"And I'll put up more sticks, too."

The sticks are the sharply pointed mini spears that are used for making shish kebabs. You know them. You impale a small piece of meat, then slide it down the stick, then stick on a piece of onion and slide it down the stick, then stick on another piece of onion on the stick because the first one broke apart. Then you poke yourself with the stick and say something bad.

When you are done you have a spear that could be lethal to a gnome. It is filled with meat and a few pieces of onion and peppers. You then cook it over a barbecue until the wood catches fire and you frantically wave it in the air to kill the flames until one of the pieces of meat flies off.

Then you insert the stick in your mouth, like a sword swallower, trying not to stab yourself in the back of your throat while dragging off either the meat or the onion. Then you do stab yourself and you rip the whole thing out and use your fingers to pull off whatever is still stuck to the stick.

This is the real paleo caveman diet, except the cavemen just chewed the stick.

Anyway, my wife uses the sticks to make a Viet Cong trap for the crows that are ripping up our grass. We have those chafer beetle larvae. They were laid there last year by some rotten flying creatures of nature and now they are maturing into delicacies for crows.

The crows fly in for breakfast, lunch, dinner and snacks. They rip up the grass looking for the larvae and when they find one, more crows fly in and start ripping up more grass. By the time they've finished for the day much of the lawn is not a lawn. It is a minefield after the explosions.

Then at night the raccoons come. They simply rip up the areas of grass between the holes made by the crows. No larva escapes—and nor does the grass.

My wife has covered the affected battleground with the barbecue sticks, all with their pointed ends sticking up.

She puts them in at angles, she puts them in deeply, she makes a defence against the larvae and the crows and the raccoons.

But what crow is really afraid of a stick stuck in the ground and what raccoon is afraid of anything that it can play with? So the larvae wiggle below the sticks, which the crows and raccoons use for markers to know where to find them.

Before the beetles there was the moss. It rains a lot here and moss likes the rain. Every spring I try to rake out the moss but I have never succeeded. By summer there is some grass growing between the patches of moss.

That is when I borrow my neighbour's lawn mower to cut the grass.

I have a push mower that I got to lose weight. It did not work. The mower worked but I didn't. That is because it takes a great deal of effort to push a push mower. My neighbour Caroline felt bad for me last year and said I could borrow her motor mower.

So I did. Then I hit a rock with the blade and it did not sound good. I turned over the mower to see what damage I had caused.

The blade was okay. I rolled the mower back to its working position and pulled the cord. Bang. Rattle. It started with a bang and a rattle, misfiring and making a noise that the manufacturers would not use in a commercial.

And immediately it belched black smoke, shooting out the back of the mower like an old, badly neglected diesel truck hauling a heavy load up a long hill—only worse, because there was no hill and no truck. Just me and a mower and my neighbours coming to look.

I shut off the mower. This was not good, but I figured some oil had gotten into the cylinder and it would burn off, so I pulled the cord again. Bang. Rattle. Smoke. Black ugly smoke. Then *phsss*—the sound of a dying engine.

I waited for Caroline to come home. Her husband, Perry, asked if I had turned it over.

"Well, yes. To see if I'd ruined the blade."

I avoided saying "your" blade.

"You can't turn over that mower. Look. It says on the side, 'Do not turn over.'"

This I did not know.

The next day he took it to the mower fixer shop and a week later he got it back. I wanted to pay for it, but since it was old and needed fixing anyway he said no. He is a very nice guy.

I did pay for half of it and told him I would never borrow it again.

He said of course I should, and now that I had paid for part of it I should use it whenever I wanted—which I did a few days later, with more guilt flowing out of me than sweat. And when I was through cutting I went to the gas station and filled a jerry can with gasoline and then went home and filled the mower with gas, until it overflowed. And the gas spilled into a hollowed recess in the metal housing and the only way to get it out was to turn over the mower.

Which I could not do. So I mopped up the gas with a rag, and tried to wring it out back into the jerry can, which I could not. So I had gasoline soaking into the grass, which I did not tell my wife about.

The rain probably saved me, and the grass. Winter and spring came and the beetles came, and the barbecue sticks. And the moss is worse.

But when we came home from the Flower & Garden Show in Seattle we were inspired. The problem with the show is we have a real garden, the kind most people have. It's not a show garden. That is why we go to garden shows—to pretend.

Is This Us?

This is very sad. Don't read it. Seriously. You will have to face yourself as you may someday be and that is not nice.

That sounds odd. It sounds either philosophical or stupid but it doesn't sound good.

First, go to a nursing home. I am in the process of visiting someone in a nursing home and I've been doing this for years. She is a family member. She falls asleep in her wheelchair on the way to the bathroom. She doesn't remember if she had lunch five minutes after she had lunch. She asks where her great-grandchildren live, and then asks again, and again.

Down the hallway there is another woman in a wheelchair holding a doll. She runs her fingers through the doll's hair and smiles. Then she squeezes the doll and smiles again. She has not said a word in a year. Her husband goes to the home every day and sits by her side. He talks to her. She doesn't talk to him.

Waiting to eat dinner is a man who is quite young, maybe in his late forties. He has a smile. He looks pleasant. He is pleasant.

He crosses his legs, then uncrosses them, then crosses them again.

"How are you?" I ask.

"Fine," he says.

I almost think he is just nervous and is visiting someone.

"Have you been here long?" I ask, meaning this afternoon.

"Five years," he says.

Then he crosses his legs again.

"It's almost dinner," he says.

Then he uncrosses his legs.

None of these people are the people they were just a few years ago. Many of these people were us just a few years ago.

They started fading, so slowly that no one noticed, not even themselves. They forgot something. We all forget things. They got confused. We all get confused. They told a joke and could not remember the punchline. We all do this from time to time. It isn't so much that we forget the punchline; it's just that we didn't tell it right and those listening didn't get it.

"What I mean is he went down the ladder, not up the ladder. Wait. No, he went up the ladder. Yes, that's it. You get it now? I'm sorry. I always get that mixed up."

A year or so earlier, when he made up the joke, everyone laughed. What happens to us?

We don't know, including the husband who sits with his wife who doesn't talk and who holds the doll. He doesn't know what happened, how it happened or even exactly when it happened. He just sits there, every day, with his wife.

It doesn't happen to everyone, but there is the veteran who charged onto the beach with his rifle and was brave and strong and young and helped save the world. Now he doesn't recognize his son who comes every week to visit.

Meanwhile there are the friends of the veteran who were with him on the beach and they still meet for coffee and talk politics and joke about the old days. Sometimes they visit their friend in the home. Same background, same race, same religion, same finances, same diet, and so what? None of that seems to matter. It happens or it does not happen and we don't know why.

I told you not to read this.

We never know if the one who loses everything is us. We don't even know it when it becomes so. Only those who keep their minds know when someone else has lost theirs.

A baby does not know it is a baby. Someone sitting in a wheelchair staring at a wall does not know the wall is there.

As I said, this is depressing. The only reason I am writing it is because I live with it and have for years. This is not looking for sympathy. So many, many are doing what I and my wife are doing.

It is just to say to those in this world who are living with those in another world, those in the other world know you are there even if they don't say it or acknowledge it or even hint at it. Even if they are not sure who you are, they know you, or at least they know someone is there. And you are making it easier for them, just as cuddling a baby makes it easier for them.

The husband with the wife holding the doll is not just living out his wedding vows; he is giving someone who has nothing everything, and that is a very good thing.

No more about this.

No Graffiti

Of you walk along Main Street between 25th and 27th Avenues you will see no graffiti. If this is not so and you do see some, come back tomorrow. It will be gone. That is because Bryan Dyck will hunt it down and make it disappear.

Bryan is one of my favourite people. He did what we all wish for and does what most of us would never do. Here's the story:

Long ago, in the age of hippies, Bryan was a printer in Vancouver. He had long hair. He was a free and easy, tall, thin child of either the universe or 4th Avenue, which is where all the children of the universe in Vancouver hung out.

It's funny, but if you went on an archaeological dig along 4th Avenue now you would find no trace of the counterculture that thrived there. It is now a trendy stretch of fashion stores and bike shops and outdoor apparel, along with some very upscale groceries and wine shops. The ghost of a hippie would die before going there now.

Anyway, Bryan was a hippie and this was in the era when the

government was trying to bring metric to the good people of Canada. It did not want to be the only other country besides the US where folks counted by twelves and used their feet to measure space.

How the US runs most of the biggest of everything in the world and still does not have the metric system is a tribute to their ingenuity. How far is that from here? It's 12 inches to a foot, 5,280 feet to a mile and 25 miles to a gallon. What's a gallon? What's a foot? And if you don't have a ruler you can guess what an inch is by closing your pinkie and using the length between your middle knuckle and the knuckle before your fingernail.

In truth, I grew up with the knuckle measurement and it is so ingrained in my head that I still can't picture what a centimetre is. And Celsius makes no sense to me. But I know one knuckle is an inch.

And that is one reason I am still working and Bryan is not.

Bryan took one look at the metric system and said, "It is good," or something like that.

It made sense and it was simple and since he was a printer he made a thin pamphlet explaining the system of ten. This was before computers, of course, so he actually used paper and ink.

And he used pictures, photos like those in high school yearbooks. There were pictures of him holding up ten fingers, and pouring one litre of water and stuff like that, which made understanding metric simple. We should have had more hippies as teachers.

Bryan sold his pamphlets for a dollar back when a dollar was paper and was worth a dollar. He was known as the Metric Man.

But he got lucky, and in a way that could happen to you if only you did something that attracted the luck.

A reporter saw the pamphlet, interviewed Bryan and wrote a story about it for a Canadian news service. Then the big luck came. Someone in the US saw the story and since that country was thinking—not thinking very hard, but thinking—about going metric Bryan wound up on a US television talk show.

He was there only a few minutes, but it was enough for him to sell a warehouse full of pamphlets.

He made enough money to retire. He moved to Hawaii for a while and then came back to Vancouver and Main Street where his wife opened a small consignment store.

Bryan was and still is very dedicated to his wife and the store and the street where it is. Although he is still a rich man he puts on coveralls every morning and grabs a couple of cans of paint and searches for graffiti.

"The graffiti folks are cowards," he says. "They do their work in the dark and ruin someone else's property."

Bryan hunts down the sprayed initials and ugly markings and paints over them. "The way to get rid of graffiti is to make it disappear," he says, and he says it often.

The graffiti bums like to see their work. If it is not there for them to gloat over or brag about they eventually go away. It is not easy, but it works.

And then Bryan picks up the litter along the street, including the curb. And then in the spring and summer he plants flowers in the dirt at the base of the trees that struggle to live along the street.

And through it all he is friendly, smiling and never bitter about the cigarette butts or the paper that gets dropped or even the graffiti. He just makes his part of the world better.

The only thing he can't change is that paint in Canada is sold by the gallon. The manufacturers don't want to lose the US market, so when Bryan goes to the paint store, like all of us, he has to buy a can that holds 3.79 litres or one US gallon.

Go to Main Street some morning and talk to the Metric Man with his gallon of paint. You may be inspired to retire early or change part of the world—not bad no matter how you measure it.

A Young Cyclist and an Old Clock

little further up Main Street, at 22nd Avenue, is a rain-worn homemade sign. It reads "A-1 Cycle."

You cannot see bicycles when you look in the front window. The window is filled with living, breathing leaves.

"I've had that plant for twenty years," said John Quon. "And that one for thirty-seven."

He loves his plants. The thirty-seven-year-old one he got when he opened the store. Behind them are rows of bicycles, so many you really can't walk through the shop.

"Half are for sale, half for repair," he said. "My son can fix anything."

Now a couple of things: in my past life I visited this shop four or five times. Each time I came away with a wonderful story.

1) John started the shop after running a grocery store for, well, forever. He and his wife wanted something where they could take off a day. "You can't leave food alone, but bicycles are different."

He opened the store long before bikes were like Starbucks and sushi. He struggled.

2) One time I saw the grandfather, son and grandson working in the same shop. The grandson was playing with tires. Recently I went back and learned he is in university. What happened?

That line is only there for me to be amazed at.

3) I met O'Neal there. O'Neal rides every day. He rides to the top of Mount Seymour and then flies down. On the same day he will ride to the top of Cypress Bowl and then catapult down. Okay, he stays on the road, but the image is great. Between these rides he works. I don't know exactly what he does but it is indoors and he shuffles paper and he does not like being indoors.

O'Neal has only one name. O'Neal. He remembers all his friends' birthdays and calls them while he is on the road. You can hear the wind screaming past the phone on his chest while he rides. I don't know if that's illegal or not but it is a thrill to get called by O'Neal on your birthday.

In the rear of A-1 Cycle shop, John's son Rob keeps track of O'Neal's mileage. Kilometreage doesn't have the same ring to it, but he has cycled over a million kilometres. Super neat story.

4) I was working with cameraman Jim Fong in my new life . . . but let me digress for a minute. Remember the title of this book? *None of This Was Planned.*

That was the choice of the publisher, Howard White. As I've said before, he is quite a guy. He drove a bulldozer to support his dream of publishing. Dirty hands, dirty clothes in the world of publishing. Neat guy. Good story.

But honestly, I did not think the title was very good when he told me. It's too long and what the heck does not planning have to do with this? I did not like it.

He said he decided on the title after reading the first few pages. "What do you know?" I thought.

I wanted: *This Is My Last Book.*

He said, "*No.* Suppose you change your mind."

I said, "But I have nothing to say."

He said, "Trust me."

I am glad I am not a girl. Can you imagine how many times they hear that?

Anyway, I was with Jim Fong and passing by A-1 and I said, "That is a neat shop."

He replied, "My brother-in-law owns it."

"What? Stop."

We did not plan that.

Past the plants, past the bikes, "Hello Mr. Quon." Jim is very polite. "I would never call him by his first name," he said.

We pass the senior Mr. Quon and go in the back where Rob is spinning a wheel to see where it is out of alignment.

"What's new?" asks Jim.

That is the world's second most universal question, after "How are you?" First health then news.

Jim skipped the first question because he could see Rob was healthy. Also they had had dinner together a few nights earlier.

"Nothing," says Rob.

That is world's most universal answer to the second most universal question.

"Wait," he said to his brother-in-law, and he rushed into the showroom, which is packed with bikes, because his father was climbing on a stepladder. His father is nimble but at eighty-seven he should keep his feet on the ground, don't you think? His father doesn't.

"I have to wind the clock," said his father.

The old, dark wood clock with a pendulum is hanging on the wall so high up it needs to be fed by a giant or someone on a ladder.

John is up to the top, where you should not stand, and has

opened the front glass of the clock and is turning a key, which he has brought up with him.

"It's old," he said.

What is old? That is me thinking philosophically.

"It's over a hundred years old," said John, who was now coming down.

Luckily for me, Jim—that again is John's son's brother-in-law—has his camera on his brother-in-law's father. Relationships are beautiful.

The clock was bought by John's grandfather. Wow! In Canada. Of course, it looks Canadian, the kind of Canadian you see in museums, not in bike shops.

Then John inherited it, and when John went to China, long ago, he took the clock with him.

Then John came back to Canada and when he did he brought the clock back with him.

"So it has been across the ocean twice," said John.

It hung there on the wall and we could all hear it going tick, tick, etc. It connected so much together without anything being said.

And there was another story from the A-1 Cycle shop.

Smile or Not

We who write the news do not create the news.

Okay, sometimes we do.

Do not. Do so. Not. So!

I have heard that all my working life. And all that time I have said, with just a tinge of defiance and anger and hostility and controlled nastiness, "No. We do not."

I fully believe that. If you see two people dead on the street from bullets or cars or explosions, they are just that, two people dead on the street from something.

On the other hand, some reporters try to make things sound better, and some worse, just like real people.

If two people—men, women, kids, doesn't matter—are gossiping about someone else they could say, "He's a bum. He did something really bad and I hate him," or they could say, "He's got a bum rap and I don't believe he did anything bad. I kind of like him."

That is the way of life. Reporters on the other hand try to keep their feelings out of it—unless they are human.

Today, February 22, 2016, I saw a fellow downtown trying to get a dog to move. He was not doing well. The dog would not move.

This is beautiful. This is life. The immovable force meets the force that wants it to move.

I have a Chinese print on a wall in my house. It has been there for thirty years. It's a picture of a large immovable water buffalo pulling backwards against a little kid who has a rope through a ring in its nose.

The kid has the advantage because the ring would hurt but the buffalo has size and strength and is apparently accustomed to having his nose in pain.

No one wins. That's life, I say to anyone who asks, and most do ask because the print is right by the front door and you can't help seeing it if you are coming or going.

The dog and the man I saw today were the same. It is kind of funny, an eternal struggle between two opposing forces.

The difference was the man was big and the dog was small, which made the sight of it funny, at least to me and I believed to anyone else who likes to watch the big guy losing to the small guy.

"Can we take your picture," etc. You know the rest of it.

"Yes, of course, but just the dog, not me," he said.

That always takes some discussion. "But we need you. And you will make others feel good."

Then the agreement.

Of course I want the fellow there because that is what is humorous, unless you are the fellow.

He is dog sitting for a friend. He is being kind. He took the dog out for a walk. That's nice, but now the dog does not want to go home.

The dog is a mini bulldog. It is strong. It is determined.

"I'll have to carry it," says the fellow.

Wonderful, I think. The perfect ending for a story about a dog that will not walk.

Just then the dog takes a few steps.

"He's walking!" says the fellow.

Then he stops and the man picks up the malingering purebred and walks away.

It is nice, but a little weak for a story, I think. Then at the same time not far away we see a woman trying to fly a kite. She is failing. There is no wind.

She runs, but is really just dragging the kite behind herself.

This is good, too. Two people who can't get done what they want to do. It is something we all deal with once in a while.

We talk, she says she is trying out several kites because she works in a toy store that sells them and she wants to be able to tell customers what's up.

She tries again and fails again—and again and again.

"If I were a kid I'd give up and say, 'Mom, I don't want to do this,'" she says.

A breeze comes up, just a little one, and she runs again and this time the kite goes up; not far, not long, but up. Then it crashes back down. She tries once again and . . . plop. Nothing.

That is all we need, I think. Two stories of human failure. Two things that everyone can relate to. Two things that did not go the way they were supposed to go. It is like watching someone slip on a banana peel. It's funny, right? Okay, it's not if it is you.

Later I am in the edit room where truth and honesty get searched for in the pictures.

"It's funny," I tell Sabrina Gans, the editor. "It is what we all go through."

She puts the pictures together. We watch.

After a series of failures with dog and kite, the last pictures in the story are of the kite being carried by the woman and the dog being carried by the man.

Sabrina is watching the work she has put together. She is quiet. That is not good. You know the saying; if you can't say something nice don't say anything at all. Sabrina is saying nothing.

"Actually, it is not funny," I say. That is not uplifting. "Even if you can relate to it that doesn't make you feel good," I say.

"No, it doesn't," says Sabrina.

Sabrina has two small children at home. In raising them she tries to encourage them to be the best that they can be without taking away from the truth of who they are. Her editing is the same.

I think of one of my most favourite lines in all my favourite lines in rock and roll songs: "Take a sad song and make it better."

It was in a Beatles song written by Paul McCartney, who scribbled out the words to cheer up John Lennon's son after Lennon had abandoned him and his mother for a new love, Yoko Ono.

Five-year-old Julian did not understand most of what the song was about, but he could hear the message to take something bad and make it better.

That was nice. The only trouble was he didn't hear his own name because Paul McCartney thought it sounded better to say "Hey Jude" rather than "Hey Julian."

Some music historians say he changed it because Julian was sometimes used instead of Judas, which was a secret name for heroin, and he didn't want that allusion.

That came after "Lucy in the Sky with Diamonds," which everyone was sure secretly meant LSD, even if the Beatles denied it.

But this is such a side note. I wasn't thinking of any of that, only trying to take something sad and make it better.

"Suppose we ended with the dog walking and the kite flying," I said.

Sabrina said, "That's good."

"That's good" sounds better than silence.

Failure, failure, failure, then success, even if the kite only flew for a few seconds and the dog only walked for a few feet.

Perfect.

"How about adding something more positive," I said.

I took the microphone and after the first picture of the dog not walking I said, "But you have to believe."

And after the first picture of the kite not flying I said the same thing.

In the end the kite flew and the dog walked. So much better than slipping on a banana peel or watching the person fall.

We had success, something we all hope for. We took a sad song and made it better. Which was the true story? What really happened? How much did we change reality, or not? How much did Sabrina not wanting it to be down have to do with lifting it up? Everything.

Like all stories, like all life and all dinners and report cards and trips on buses, it is how you look at it that counts. The kite flew. The dog walked. And that is the truth.

Randy Tait

*N*ow here is a guy who took a sad song and made it into an opera, and not one of those traditional ones where everyone dies at the end. It is an opera in which the whole town is cheering the hero who has just slain the dragon.

Except Randy Tait has never been to an opera.

However, he is really good as Frosty the Snowman. If you go to Burnaby Village Museum at Christmas you can see him, a giant snowman waving at kids and having his picture taken with them and waddling around with pretend pieces of coal on his smiling snow-white face.

Under the costume he is not white, but he does have a smile.

When I first met him he wasn't smiling. He had a stern face, with some bruises and unwashed hair.

He had just gotten out of prison. He had spent years there. Between trips back and forth living in a cage he lived in the back alleys of the Downtown Eastside.

"I remember waking up without a shirt surrounded by broken glass," he said. "If I had rolled over I would have bled to death."

Sad songs happen but somewhere, somehow, in some mysterious way he said to himself he had to do something. He had to make it better or he would die—and his death would not even be noticed.

On the day I met him I was standing on the steps of the Carnegie Centre just looking for something, as always.

He climbed the steps. We nodded, said a hello that was less than one syllable, followed by "How 'r' you?", which led to him saying he was going to an AA meeting but that he didn't know if he could last through the whole thing.

I wished him luck, of course, the same as you would do for anyone facing anything hard.

I saw him a few more times over the next year or two and each time he was better, cleaner, straighter, stronger and talking more.

"I am doing this for me," he said, which is the most important thing anyone changing their life has to learn.

Jump ahead a little over a decade from that first meeting. Randy had called me to say he was going back up those steps at the centre for a celebration.

I waited across the street with a cameraman. Randy, looking like a giant in neat fitting clothing and polished shoes, was going to share his eleven-year sobriety cake.

"This is the best day since the last best day," he said.

He is Native. "Most people did not expect I could do this. They think we can't control ourselves. I'd like to meet them," he said.

As we crossed the street several of the citizens of Main and Hastings came to say hello to him. "He is a legend," said one of them.

Looking at Randy, I thought the tiny telephone receiver stuck in his ear looked out of place for a tough guy on the skids.

"I get calls from people who need to talk," he said.

Then he touched his ear. The phone had been ringing. Randy talked, then said to the person who called that he would talk again very soon. Then he touched his ear again. Another call.

He would turn it off just for the cake and then turn it back on.

The last time I saw him was at the Native New Year's celebration at the PNE and he was fully dressed in his aboriginal finest. He said he had to leave early the next morning to fly to Powell River to give a talk on preventing teenage suicide.

All he did was something so simple. He took a sad song and did you know what to it. He made it better. It works all the time.

A Famous Dog Story

I do not like the rain. Only crazy people are out and it is hard to talk to them because they all want to tell me how much they like the rain.

Other people are out, too, such as joggers, who are crazy because they run in the rain. They may be getting healthy but they are also getting wet and then they could get sick.

"How come you got sick?"

"I was trying to get healthy."

What's more, joggers are running too fast for me to say, "Excuse me, it is none of my business, but why are you running—or wearing that silly hat, or have no shoes, which is getting popular and is crazy, or have you done something amazing like run a million kilometres or something that we could put on television?"

I cannot ask that because they are gone before I can finish saying "Excuse me . . ." The very few that do stop still keep running in place while I'm talking and it's hard to talk to someone who is bouncing up and down, and when they realize that they would have to stop running to answer my request they mostly shake their heads and go back to running, which is always away from me.

And I don't like dog walkers, because they are always walking in the rain and when I ask why are they doing that they usually hold up a plastic bag containing something dogs must think people cherish because people are always collecting it and keeping it after the dog is finished with it. That must go beyond the understanding of even very smart dogs.

Anyway, dog walkers in the rain were not what I was looking for.

But then, way down near the water at Sunset Beach I saw some people. They were just standing, in the rain. This is good, I think. Except they are way, way down there, and that is bad.

I walk and walk. The rain is coming sideways and my umbrella is growing weak but the people are not moving so we have a chance. There are two of them I can now see.

When I get almost within shouting distance they start to walk away.

"Wait," I beg.

One of them starts walking faster. Who wouldn't when it's raining and someone on the beach whom you don't know wants you not to go?

They have on long dresses, which are soaked. I cannot tell what race or nationality these people are, but they are wet.

"Excuse me, it's none of my business, but can you tell me what you are doing here?"

I tried not to sound like the secret police, but who else would be stopping them on the beach in the rain?

One kept walking.

"We were praying," said the other one.

This was wonderful. I love people who pray. It is so heavenly and earthly and everything in between.

I once saw a man playing the bagpipes near the edge of the ocean. There were others with him. They were spreading the ashes of a friend and listening to the pipes, which were the favourite of the man who had become the ashes, and they were praying for him. In the world of beauty, this was beautiful.

Yes, we could take pictures of them. They thought it was good for honouring their friend. They, like cavemen and Egyptians and Romans and modern Christians, Jews, Muslims and others, were trying to connect with something no one has ever connected with.

Another time I saw a lone Chinese restaurant worker in a back alley off Pender Street. He was wearing his apron as he squatted over a pot with a fire. Into the pot he was putting paper, which I knew was make believe money that you can buy in any Chinese shop. He was sending it to someone in another world.

There were no words exchanged, there could not be, but the picture was better than words. I explained what he was doing for those who did not know and then we just watched. To me there was nothing more wonderful or beautiful or meaningful. We try to do what we can do in the only way we can do it.

I have told these stories many times. You don't need a TV to see them.

And now there was a woman at the edge of the sea in the rain praying. It could not be better.

"Could we take a picture of you?"

She nodded.

Heaven had opened its gates.

I looked at Todd, the cameraman. Yes, I nodded, praying that his camera had its personal rain jacket, which all of them have but none of them fit and they are a pain to put on and take off and all the camera people hate them, but if you don't have it and the camera gets wet it stops.

He nodded. There was a lot of nodding going on, which was good.

Then the other woman, who was walking away, said something to the woman who had said Yes and I knew that the other woman had said No.

"Sorry, we have to go," said the woman who had said Yes that was now No.

And they walked away, in the rain.

Darn.

Todd and I started walking back to the parking lot where he hoped he had not gotten a ticket. He had been in such a rush to get to the women who he did not know were praying that he hadn't paid for parking.

According to the rules of the television station, they will pay for all parking but not for parking tickets.

They, the people who make those rules, know nothing, nothing at all, about how the product that they are selling gets collected. In short, people in management live in a comfortable world.

We will leave that aside.

Back to the rain and the beach. We were still walking. The prospects looked dim. No, actually they looked wet and barren and empty and impossible and it was late and there is just so much time allotted to finding something before it gets economically unworkable.

There is camera time, editing time and just plain time when some producer inside says, "If those hard-working people (meaning those useless idiots who can't do their job) outside don't come up with something we will have to find something else to put in that slot."

There must be *something*, I said to me.

And there was a man with a dog. No. I am not going to talk to him. No. Not. No, I refuse. He is walking a dog in the rain. So what? I don't care.

"Hello," he says.

How can you resist an invitation like that?

"Hello," I say. "Nice dog."

I didn't mean it.

"He's an international celebrity," said the man.

"What do you mean?" I asked, desperately.

I could hear it in my own voice. That was not a question, it was a plea. Please say something good.

"Well," he said, and then he went into a long, long story about their last dog dying and he and his wife wanting a new dog but then discovering how free life was without a dog.

"We could go to movies and plays and out for dinner without worrying about our dog."

Wonderful, I thought. Boring, I thought. The rain is hitting me, I didn't even have to think.

We looked at his dog wandering across the sand where you are not supposed to let dogs go free.

"We found him on the internet."

Good, I thought. Like internet dating. Don't care.

"He was in Mason City, Iowa."

Amazing, I thought. I really did think that. It is a good beginning—not much to go on after that, but a good beginning.

"But we couldn't fly back with him."

This is where I go "Huh?"

"They didn't want him to fly. It might be bad because he was so small."

That is good; better than good, I thought.

He kept talking.

"So my wife and father-in-law drove down to pick him up."

That is pretty good. I know Iowa is in the middle of the US. Long drive.

Then came a monologue about how he, the fellow with the dog, had had a passport but it had been due to expire in a few months so he couldn't go but he wished he'd been able to because, "Don't tell anyone, but I am a much better driver than my wife or father-in-law."

Sigh.

Then he said, "Apparently nothing happens in Mason City, Iowa, because a reporter showed up when my wife and her father went to the shelter."

Wow!

"They did a story about the 'international adoption' and we were on the nightly news."

Super wow!

Pictures of the dog, named Chester. Pictures of the owner, named Derek.

No pictures of Chester emptying his bowels on the beach or of Derek making a trek to find the leavings or of me directing him to the sizable leavings because Chester now weighed 125 pounds.

But there was something—an international dog.

I went back to the people who work indoors in the television station and told them what the story was about: an international dog.

Somehow we would make it exciting, I said, with a prayer they did not hear. See, prayers are everywhere.

This goes on every day, so when I tell you to find something interesting to tell to someone else I am giving you a hard job, sometimes an impossible task. Nonetheless the search is sometimes, just sometimes, worth the effort.

I got to my computer but I had no idea how to look up Chester the dog on the internet. I am more than a generation or two removed from the people of today. I am an alien with a ballpoint pen and a library card.

I figure we can still do the story with just the fellow's description of how much publicity the dog got and how they had to drive to get him.

It would work, I prayed.

I stepped into the dark edit room. There was Carl, who did not strike me as a happy person until he went on vacation and met a girl. She was from Ohio.

"Here is her picture," he said.

He was happy. It is like I said in the beginning of this book, love has everything to do with everything. Don't question it. Just suffer through it. It will give you everything you want, and take away everything you have.

It is powerful.

Carl was happy.

I mentioned the television story on the fellow with the dog. Then I took a sip of my tea.

This has been a disaster with me. I used to drink coffee. Then I got older—too old to write a book and too old to make it to the bathroom when I drink coffee.

So I drink tea. It has the same effect but milder. I can make it to the bathroom. Don't expect getting older will be easy.

When I got back Carl had up on the screen a five-year-old television news story from Mason City, Iowa. How did he do that? I had tried and failed when I got back to the television station. I had no idea how to do it.

Carl, like the other editors, did something impossible, at least to me. It is mind boggling. And then I looked at the monitor.

There was the Mason City anchor who looked like he was in high school (okay, I am prejudiced) introducing the story about the "international adoption" and then cut to a reporter who looked like a Grade 12 classmate.

And nothing could be better. This was small town television news. This was the real thing.

Put that in the story, the young anchor reading a teleprompter that said, "Pet adoptions are not unusual in Mason City, but an international one is."

And then the reporter on the scene, saying, "Today, someone from far-off Canada is picking up cute little Chester," over pictures of cute little Chester.

A tag line written across the screen, over cute Chester romping around, says, "Canada bound."

It was big news in Mason City, but the best news was for me.

The old video of the young anchor and reporter made the story wonderful. At the end I said he was an international star, or something like that.

It really doesn't matter what I said. The story was made by using pictures that Carl found and I could say, My gosh, they thought it was a big deal that the dog was coming to far-away Canada.

In truth, the anchor and reporter were more memorable than the dog.

And in truth, the big, big boss wrote to me on Facebook that the footage from Iowa was fantastic. I wrote back saying it was Carl the editor who found it.

That is probably why I love people who walk their dogs in the rain—and editors who are in love, even just briefly.

The Poor Dog

One more dog in the rain story. We did not have to hunt for this one.

We had stopped on a downtown street between one large condo and another large condo. We stopped just to look. The windshield wipers were still going and we could see the people moving like fish in a bowl.

Then along came the well-dressed woman walking her dog. I say walking, but actually the dog never touched the ground. She had it under her arm, which was small, but not as small as the dog.

It was a perfect downtown dog—tiny, with a tiny woof. She came out of a condo and walked halfway up the street to where there was a patch of artificial grass in front of a coffee shop.

Once upon a time there was a great forest in this same spot. Now there is concrete and plastic grass. If anyone wonders why the earth is falling apart and the oceans are rising and the glaciers are melting and the weather is changing, just look at the plastic grass and the concrete.

But that was not the concern of the woman. She only wanted her little house pet to do something so she could get back to work.

She put the small thing down on the grass that was not grass and held onto the leash, which had shiny emeralds embedded in it.

The small thing sniffed, took two or three steps, then squatted and did something. But that was not enough doing for the woman at the end of the shiny emeralds. She tugged on the leash and pulled the small thing to another part of the make-believe ground.

There the tiny thing with legs and a tail sniffed again, circled twice, squatted again and did the rest of the thing that the woman was waiting for.

She took out a plastic bag and picked up the stuff, both tiny deposits (no doubt still warm), gathered up the little creature in one arm and started to walk away.

"Excuse me, it's none of my business, but does your dog ever see real grass?" I asked.

She looked at me with confusion. Should she answer? Should she call the police? Should she run?

"Why?" she said.

"I was just wondering if she ever gets to walk on real grass."

"No. That would be dirty," said the woman. "I have expensive carpeting and I want to keep it clean. Good day."

She walked away, back through the front door of the condo and disappeared.

I was hoping that in a few minutes the little thing would stretch out on those expensive carpets—and fart.

ManWoman

Sometimes you just gotta do what you gotta do.

Even if it's crazy and it will cost you dearly and you can't undo it. Even if the reason for it is hard to explain and most would not believe it.

ManWoman. It has been years since I last wrote about him. If you know who I am talking about you will say, "Oh, yeah, there was a real nutcase." And then you will tell someone the story.

If you don't know him, a few moments from now you will say, "Wow, there was a real nutcase." And then you will tell someone the story.

On the other hand it is one of those stories with no moral uplift. It is just weird and shocking and sometimes it is good to read about someone who has the courage to do what he wants to do even if the rest of the world, and that is no exaggeration, wants him to hide or go away or at least wear long sleeves and a face mask.

ManWoman was born Patrick Kemball in Cranbrook. It is a

pretty town near the Alberta border. He described himself as a "normal, beer-guzzling, girl-chasing, car-crazy Canadian youth."

He studied engineering, but he liked art and was good at it. Then he had a dream. He has never said what he was eating or reading or doing the night before but he swore there were no drugs involved. In his dream a glowing figure in a white robe came to him and told him it was his mission to revive the good name of the swastika.

Well, right there, that is where I quit. Right at that moment, when he told me that, I thought please give me an easier job, like bringing world peace or getting the sugar out of soda pop.

But no, the glowing figure wanted the reputation of the world's most hated symbol cleaned and polished.

So Patrick did what he thought he had to do: he got a tattoo, just a tiny one, of a swastika on his pinky.

His mother, who was Jewish, thought this was odd. His aunt and her daughter, who had tattoos of numbers on their arms from a bad time in a concentration camp in Poland, thought this was not the best of ideas.

And then Patrick had another dream. Actually, it was the same dream but another night. He got another tattoo of the same symbol. Only this time it was larger and on his arm. He looked a little scary on the quiet streets of Cranbrook, which was trying to attract tourists.

Jump ahead a few years to the time when I met him. By then he had two hundred tattoos, each a little different in style and size, but all swastikas.

Several times people threatened to beat him into the ground. Once an older Jewish man hit him with a cane. Every time he went through an airport security check he was checked, and then checked again.

He was a big man, he had long hair and he wore coveralls—bright yellow coveralls. When he walked on a crowded street he usually had plenty of room.

"Why?" I obviously asked.

"Because it is my mission," he said.

"But," I tried to add without saying that this is crazy.

"There are no buts," he said. "You gotta do what you gotta do so I am doing it."

He then went into the history of the swastika, which for thousands of years was a good symbol.

He had a picture of a turn-of-the-century Canadian women's ice-hockey team with a swastika on each of their sweaters. They lived in Swastika, Ontario, which is now part of a place called Kirkland Lake, which is easier to say.

He told me, and everyone else who would listen, that in many ancient civilizations the symbol meant good luck.

And then he had another dream.

Women were not being treated equally and he should do something about it.

He did. He legally changed his name to ManWoman.

This would cause problems with the tax people and the census.

"Mr. Woman, what is your first name?"

Much of his art contained swastikas, but instead of jackboots and tanks surrounding them, ManWoman painted doves and bunny rabbits.

In the end, I don't think he won. The ugly symbol of the broken cross is too deeply scarred into our lives. The pain and death and destruction that went with it will take a long time to ease.

Maybe in a thousand years. Or maybe more.

But as for ManWoman, he did what he said he had to do, and he did it with a courage that was unbeatable. If only we had that courage, just with a different symbol, think of what we could do.

Sadly, after I did the story it sat on a shelf in the back of the edit rooms for months before someone finally ran it, at the end of the late show on a holiday Saturday night when there was a tiny audience.

ManWoman died a few years ago. Bone cancer, according to the doctors. Ink poisoning, according to his brother.

Baseball

It is time for something happy, and that is baseball.

I know some of you are groaning.

"Baseball is slow. Baseball is tedious. Nothing happens in baseball."

That is three of you talking. But you are all wrong, along with the other three thousand who agree with you.

You like hockey or football or soccer or badminton—anything but baseball. Silly people.

True baseball is not what it once was, but if you grew up with it you could forgive it now for generally being a two-person game. There is the trillionaire pitcher who is only expected to last half the game before a reliever comes in to let the star's arm rest. And of course the reliever is only expected to last a few more innings before the closer comes in all fresh to do what the other two so far have not done and win the game.

And there is the batter who swings, stops, loosens his gloves and then tightens his gloves, kicks the dirt, steps into the batter's box and then watches a pitch go by that anyone could see was perfect. Then he steps out of the box, loosens his gloves, tightens his gloves, kicks the dirt and then steps back into the box.

For this, each year, he gets the average person's lifetime salary. Okay, you have a point. I agree with you, that's boring.

But on the other hand, I was telling the editor, James Buck, about a magazine I once had from the Smithsonian Institution in Washington, DC. It had a cover story on old-time baseball as it was played in the 1870s and '80s.

No gloves. There were many things different, but most of all no gloves. Because of that many balls were dropped or missed. Because of that there were many base runners and because of that the scores were high. How about 25–22, or higher? Now that would keep you awake.

Today's gloves stick out a foot past the hand, which makes catching impossible balls commonplace, which keeps the runners from running, which adds to the lack of something happening.

So again, I agree with you.

And then James sent me the link to a YouTube video of the revival of old-time baseball, for which I gave him one of those giant thank yous, way bigger than a regular thank you.

You can find it and be fascinated. Thinner bats, funny uniforms and extreme fun in playing. Now that is baseball.

And that is what I grew up with on the streets of New York. We played stickball just as often and in games that were just as wild as street hockey in Canada.

Girls, boys, everyone played. No gloves, no adult supervision, no uniforms, no scorekeeper. One ball, one broomstick and scores that were higher than your fingers could count. That is what made baseball wonderful—that and the fact that I once saw Jackie Robinson play.

I've written about this before, but if by some strange chance you missed it, here is the recap. We all skipped school. This was right before the Dodgers left Brooklyn for Los Angeles. We sat in the bleachers in Ebbets Field, a sacred place to those who loved the Dodgers but in truth it was a terribly hot place where you got bleached by the sun.

We could only see Number 42 from the back, and he was far away, but we said at that time that this would be one of the most wonderful things we ever did in our lives. We were right.

There were some men sitting in front of us drinking beer and smoking cigars and shouting a lot of insults at Jackie and Pee Wee Reese, who was his friend.

Once, during a terrible time of insults on the field when Robinson first joined the Dodgers, Pee Wee put his arm around Jackie's shoulders. It was sad that he had to do it. It was incredibly brave that he did.

As far as the ugly men in front of us went, it took some work and some ingenuity but in short we kept saying we were going to throw soda over each other and that eventually got rid of them. The second best part of that was that the only seats left were next to a section of black fans. The men were quiet for the rest of the game.

But we did get to see Jackie Robinson play. It still gives me a thrill.

And in Vancouver I have been to many Vancouver Canadians games. They are Single A, which means you don't get any lower.

From Single A you obviously go to Double A and then Triple A, and there you are starting to think that maybe there's a remote possibility you will be called up to the majors to fill in for a game. And then, who knows.

So you can see that in the Single A league the dream is far off, which only makes them play harder. The games are wonderful and so is the stadium—small enough that you can actually see the players and hear them when they miss. That's the time to cover your little kid's ears.

That is exciting baseball.

And then there was the Japanese man in the parking lot at Sunset Beach. He had white hair under his baseball cap. He had a complete uniform, including the knickers that some major league teams still wear. He had a glove and a baseball made of hard, very hard, rubber.

He wound up and pitched at a concrete traffic barrier. Bang, strike. The ball hit right in the centre of the curve of the concrete. That is not easy to do.

It came back to him on one bounce. He scooped it up and put his arms up, then twisted his body and fired out his right arm with the ball leaving his hand again with beautiful accuracy.

I hated to stop him, but I had to talk to him.

He spoke very little English. After several tries, mostly between pitches, we learned he was visiting here. He played on a seniors' team in Japan. He had brought his uniform and glove with him in case he found a game here he could play in.

And no, he was not a pitcher, although he sure was a good one. He played second base.

That's all. I just watched him. It wasn't like watching Jackie Robinson or playing stickball, but I will keep the memory just as long.

Not Even a Question

You might have seen this story, but it is worth repeating because good stories are like Christmas: they don't get old.

Elena Schwartzman was with her four kids at the Richmond Public Market. She took them for lunch in the food court. Four kids pack a lot of stuff and then there is the stuff the mother has to carry—there are toys and coats and diapers and bags and more stuff.

Plus there are the kids. They sometimes wander off, and it's terribly hard to explain leaving one of them behind!

When they had eaten, Elena got everything together and marched her kids and carried her stuff and pushed the stroller to the car.

When she got home that something happened that happens to almost everyone sometime. It was that moment when the world crashes and you look again and then it crashes much harder, because it is true.

"No, it can't be."

Back to the car to search. Maybe it's there.

No.

Under the seat. Maybe it fell.

No.

She called the market, got their lost and found and—sorry, nothing. Thank you anyway.

And then the big crash as the realization sets in. *Everything* was in her bag. It's crazy, but we all do it. Everything that is valuable we put in one place: credit cards, debit cards, cash, driver's licence, medical cards, library cards, receipts, pictures, supermarket points cards, Air Miles, BCAA.

Some carry more—citizenship card, NEXUS, lottery tickets—and all of this in a folded up piece of leather in a pocket with no zipper or button.

Unless you are a woman. Then you have your bag, which has your wallet in it as well as your cellphone and a few hundred other things that are very important.

This is not meant sarcastically. We all do it, and sometimes it just happens.

Elena remembered hooking her bag over the back of the chair she was sitting at because there was no more room on the table or on the other chairs. And the back of the chair was safe because she, as many women know, could press her back against the straps. Bag locked in.

And then she got up and packed up.

"I was trying to make sure I had all the kids," she said.

She did have them, and she had all their stuff, but she didn't notice the bag as she walked away.

After the stomach-turning discovery she left her kids with her husband and went back to the market.

"It wasn't there. I knew it wouldn't be but I had to look."

She talked to a few people selling food. She was desperate, but no, nothing.

The next day she called again.

Yes, the bag was there. Yes, she could pick it up. All the world was good again—unless, of course, there was nothing in the wallet in the bag.

She rushed to get there, as we all would, and yes, everything was there.

"Who? How?"

"I believe it was one of our custodians," said the woman in the administration office who gave her the bag.

"Which one?"

"I'll show you," the administrator said.

A Filipino man pushing a cart with cleaning supplies was the hero.

Elena walked quickly to him and thanked him. He smiled. He nodded. He felt good. She felt wonderful and she was so grateful.

Elena is from Ukraine. In her country they make a most wonderful cake with cream puffs inside and a kind of marzipan top that overflows the cake like a snug roof. It takes a long time to make.

She brought the cake to the food court and I was lucky enough to be there talking to Elena when she saw her hero cleaning some nearby tables.

"That's him! That's him," she almost shrieked.

She was bouncing. She stopped talking to me and literally ran to him.

"Remember me?" she said.

He looked, then smiled. "Oh, yes, thank you," he said.

"No, I thank *you*," she said. "You saved me."

He smiled again. She gave him the cake. He looked surprised, not knowing what he should do with it. He still had his cleaning cart and was holding a mop in one hand, but he took it and thanked her again.

He said he had seen her with her children while he was cleaning tables. The next time he got close she was gone but the bag was there.

"I didn't want to touch it," he said. "Someone might see me and that would be bad."

He stood guard over it while he used his radio to call security, which took a while to come. Meanwhile he was getting behind in his cleaning.

Eventually someone came and took the bag. He said he was happy and that was the last he thought of it. He went back to cleaning.

I talked to him. His name is Dairo. I did not expect an answer, because most people will not tell you this, but I asked him how much he made. He didn't understand the question.

"What is your salary?"

Again, he didn't get it, probably because the food fair was noisy and he didn't imagine that was what I was asking.

"How much do you get per hour?"

"Ten dollars and forty-five cents," he said.

"You gave back a bag with money in it," I said.

He looked at me again as though one of us did not understand the question, but this time it was me failing to understand that this was not a question to him. Not giving it back was an impossibility. I didn't ask him, but I know the thought of taking the bag never occurred to him.

I asked if he had a family that he could share the cake with.

He said his wife was still in the Philippines, which meant that he was working to send money to her.

I asked how long he had been in the country.

"Four months," he said.

Wow, I thought to myself. Thank goodness for the immigration officer who let him in.

Then Elena left with her bag over her shoulder. She couldn't believe someone could be so good.

And Dairo walked back to his work station with the cake. He didn't know what to do with it. He couldn't put it there, not with the used plastic forks and empty cups, so he picked a clean table and gave it an extra wipe. Then he put the cake in the centre and went back to work clearing up other people's dishes.

He would keep sending his wife money until she could join

him. He would tell her the story as soon as he could call, and I imagine she would say he did what she would have wished him to do.

He was only wishing he could share the cake with her.

Daffodils

This is weird. This is how life happens. First you think something is nothing, like turning a corner or saying hello to someone. Then the hello turns into another meeting, and that turns into coffee, which turns into coffee every week for five years. And you have something that changes your life.

Gary Tapp was waiting for a video recording disc. Gary is the chief operator of the microwave and satellite trucks. I parked near to where he was waiting and said hello.

He said to me, "Why don't you do a story about daffodils?" He had seen some blooming that morning and thought they were beautiful.

I thanked him but I didn't think that was a story. That was a picture.

Gary is on the road a great deal of the time. He is always behind the screen whenever you see a live talking head and a reporter. He is always working through the six o'clock show.

And on this day he was waiting in front of the post office, which is a tiny imitation of a post office. Can you imagine that the major mail collecting and sorting plant in British Columbia is now a parking lot for movie crews? If you buy a stamp there, which you still can do, you have to mail your letter in a mailbox. It used to be that you put it into an opening that went to the sorting room but the sorting room is no more.

No one writes letters. Fewer send Christmas cards. If it were not for bills from Hydro and Telus you would get no mail. Okay, you can still count on the god-loving industries that want to you to send them money to help others, the others of whom they send pictures.

I wrote "god-loving" in lower case, because there is no real God in their loving. They want your money. That is the only god most of them love.

On with the story. Gary Tapp was waiting for the arrival of pictures that will fill fifteen seconds of the noon show.

Cameraman Steve Murray was at the Seawall where there was a ceremony for the death of someone who was very nice. He was an ESL teacher who loved his students and they loved him. The teacher sat close to them where they could gather around. He taught them not only English but the fun of learning.

Then he was riding his bicycle on the Seawall at the moment when a homeless guy was digging through the garbage of a large bin. How does this happen? How in all the universe does a good fellow on his bike happen to ride by a lost soul who has found a chunk of metal junk and throws it out, violently, over his shoulder, in disgust because it is in the way of him finding an empty soda can?

How can it be that that piece of metal flies out over the bike path, hits the teacher in the head and knocks him off his bike and, even with a helmet on, his head hits the ground hard enough to knock the life out of him?

How does this happen? How does selfish mindlessness take over goodness and kindness? There is no answer, because we couldn't bear to hear that nothing matters and it is all a question of luck—or lack of it. We desperately want justification for why the good guy was killed by the totally random thoughtlessness of a guy who wasn't bad, just laced with self-pity and anger, but we are not going to get that justification. Living is not easy.

And then the homeless guy pulled his head out of the bin, unquestionably saw the fellow from the bicycle lying on the ground, and left.

Steve was there at a memorial organized by dozens of the dead fellow's students and friends. They all wanted to give a speech on how much he meant to them. Steve had to get a picture that could run on the noon news. It was ten-thirty a.m. and speeches don't make the news, unless it is Donald Trump being an idiot, and thankfully his speeches are short.

One speech followed another. Steve waited. It was 10:45. It doesn't take long to get pictures on the air, but it does take some time. There is the fact of taking the video, then walking, quickly, back to the truck and driving to the microwave van, taking the disc out of the camera and getting it into the machinery that transmits it. At the other end there is the receiving and cutting it down to the size that will fit into the show and then pushing the right buttons to make it happen.

Time goes by quickly if you are Steve. The brief video is scheduled to run right after noon and Steve is still with the students at eleven and they are still making speeches of how much they loved their teacher. Steve is anxious. Sadness in front of him, expediency in his head.

Time goes by slowly if you are one of the grieving students. He was a friend and you want to take your time speaking in the language he taught you. His students are reflective, but you get in borderline panic if you are holding the camera. You want to capture the sadness and meaning of the moment and you want it on the air. It is after eleven a.m. but you can still do it.

Steve has recorded a few touching farewell comments, but there is nothing to see except the balloons that will be released. Someone in the crowd says they should each write a note to their teacher and attach them to the balloons.

Fifteen minutes later they are still writing.

Panic! Steve was supposed to meet me at eleven. I can wait, but the show can't and it's a five-minute walk back to his truck in the parking lot. If he doesn't leave now none of the talks will make it, much less the release of the balloons that have not yet been released.

There will have to be a phone call to the station. You don't want to make this phone call because even if you say the event has not happened yet, by the time the message gets relayed it will be "Steve hasn't got the picture, drop the story," and whose fault is that? Well, Steve's, of course.

Then suddenly, the balloons are released and Steve shoots the video of the most touching thing the students can do for their teacher who died in a most undeserving way.

Then he runs, and the students see him running and possibly, just possibly, think that is not a polite way for the media to leave such a solemn event.

He phones, hands-free, while he drives to meet the microwave truck that would have gone to him if he had known it would be so late but he didn't know and so the truck was set up downtown.

Steve gets there just a few minutes later and hands the disc to Gary in the microwave truck. Gary puts it in a machine and feeds it to the station and presto, at 12:10 the video of the balloons is on the air along with words that tell of the tragedy.

"Daffodils," Gary says to me in a calm voice.

Steve and I leave to find something, but it will not be daffodils because I don't know where I could find them and even if I did I wouldn't know what to say about them.

We go to Queen Elizabeth Park and circle the top and bottom roads. There is nothing.

"Would you mind doing it again?" I ask.

I believe that going over the same road twice is as good as going over a new road. The second time there is a fellow playing basketball

by himself. Maybe he is trying out for the school team and is practising because he almost made it last year but did not. This year he
would.

"Nope, just killing time," he said.

Then we see a fellow playing Frisbee golf. That is not the official name—it is really called disc golf—but if I say Frisbee golf then
you have a picture of it. It can't be called Frisbee golf because of
copyrights.

By the way, just in case you don't know where it came from, the
Frisbee is one of those most wonderful stories.

In 1937 after a fellow named Fred Morrison and his girlfriend,
Lucile, had finished eating a pie on a date on a beach in Los Angeles
they began tossing the metal pie plate back and forth. They could
spin it and it was fun.

Someone offered them a quarter for the plate. Not bad, they
could buy them for a nickel. They went into business and got married.

One hitch: World War II and he was in the Army Air Force
flying propeller-driven fighter planes. Then he was shot down and
captured.

While a prisoner of war, in addition to figuring out how to escape and how to survive he thought of his pie plates. He was a pilot
and he knew what kept things in the air. With a few modifications
he could make the plates out of plastic and the spinning would cause
the lift that would make them travel much further than a pie plate.

After the war he did just that. He called the first one a Flyin-
Saucer and then after more modifications it became a Pluto Platter.
He sold them at county fairs for a dollar apiece.

Then came the biggest success of all, one of those things you cannot do on your own. Someone somewhere saw the Pluto Platter and
told someone else who told someone at the Wham-O toy company,
which bought it.

Morrison had the patent, Wham-O could mass distribute it and
everyone was happy getting rich off a spinning platter.

Then someone at Wham-O heard that kids at a college in

Connecticut were playing with the Pluto Platter but were calling it a Frisbie. The name came from the pie company that had sold their goods on metal pie platters decades earlier, when Fred and Lucile hadn't been the only ones spinning them through the air for fun. Wham-O dropped Pluto Platter and changed the name to Frisbee.

Morrison hated the name, but with the new name sales soared and Morrison soon loved the name.

So Steve pulled over and I talked to the man with the discs throwing them into a wire cage. It's a neat sport and it's free but he was just practising.

We went to the top of the park and while Steve parked I saw a couple carrying a plant. I followed them.

Why, etc? It was a gift for the woman's mother.

Wonderful but, "No," she said. Embarrassed? In a hurry? It doesn't matter, no is no.

There was a patch of daffodils near where I was getting rejected and, thinking of Gary, I looked and looked but could think of nothing to say about them.

And then I looked up at a tree very close by and there, where the tree split into two branches, was a dried and dead bouquet of roses. They were wrapped in cellophane and next to the stems of the flowers was a Kit Kat.

It was a memorial for someone whom I'll never know. It was like the balloons that Steve had photographed an hour earlier. It was something that meant so much to someone.

Someone had been in pain. Something had ended. But a few steps away something was new and beginning. It always happens. It is what religions and poems are made of but most of all it is what keeps us going—spring. Pictures of the roses and candy. Pictures of the daffodils. And one picture of both.

And of course Gary didn't see it. He was working. But thanks anyway.

Stones and the Woman

She was making a clean break with the past and that is very hard to do. Things she had collected and treasured for years she was leaving behind.

She was on the beach. So many great things happen on the beach. I think it is because it is a divide between two worlds and we get to stand on one and touch the other.

She was in both worlds. She had placed the small stones on the sand and then spread more sand from a jar around the stones.

"I got this in Hawaii," she said, holding up one stone. "And this is sand from a beach that I walked on almost every day."

"So why are you putting them here?" I asked.

She picked up another stone, looked at it and remembered something that she did not share.

"It is time to let them go," she said.

Some were from the Maritimes, where she had lived. Some were from other places that she had visited and many were from Hawaii where she spent a few years.

"In a little while the tide will come in and when it goes out it will take them with it."

She was stronger than me. I have a stone that is black and that answered a question for me and that I hold dear.

I was kind of desperate . . . gee, that's unusual . . . for a story and once again I was in Queen Elizabeth Park when I saw a man packing away his golf clubs. There is a pitch and putt course up there that is free in the winter.

I talked to him about golf but that went nowhere. Then he told me he was in a rush because he had to get back to school.

"Learning?"

"Teaching."

"What?"

"Geology."

Wonderful, I thought. Rocks. "So you know what kind of rocks these are," I said while hoping there would be something down on the ground.

"How about this whole mountain? Do you know it is one rock," he said.

Wonderful, I thought.

"A few million years ago this was a volcano. That's why it's the highest point in the city."

Oh super wonderful.

"The quarry in the middle is all that remains of the mouth of the volcano."

Not only super incredibly wonderful but there is something to take a picture of.

Then he said he had to go.

"One more thing. Please, just one. Anything."

"Okay," he said. "You know as you drive north on Cambie Street, at about 41st Avenue you see a few houses that are built on top of stone?"

I nodded.

"Black stone, like a wall," he added emphatically, like a teacher who did not want me to miss the importance of this.

I had seen the stone for years and wondered about it but I'd never done anything to find out, which is a sad thing to admit.

People say this kind of thing to me all the time and I get annoyed.

They say, "I pass by this unusual thing (fellow with a horn, woman with flowers who always sits at the same bus stop, whatever) every day and wonder what's going on. Would you please find out for me and do a story and tell me when it will air."

Seriously. At least once a week. But here I am admitting the same thing, without asking someone to find out for me. I had wondered and done nothing about it, for years. Guilty.

"That is a bit of hardened lava from the volcano. And now I have to go." And he left.

What a lesson, in less than two minutes. After taking pictures of the quarry and then going down to the bottom of the park so we could take a picture of the mountain, which now is called Little Mountain although once it was a big mountain, we went to Cambie Street and 41st Avenue.

For the houses that were built on solid black stone I now had an answer as to why. A few more pictures and we were done with a story that actually contained information.

At the base of the wall of stone there were small pieces that had broken off. They are millions of years old. I wanted to have one, but there was a problem. They might be on private property. No, they could not be. Let me see. If I were the government I would make their property end right about there, close to the house, but if I were the homeowner I would think my property ended way out here, impossibly far out here.

Somewhere in between were the stones, at the base of a wall older than the argument of making the Lions Gate Bridge four lanes.

"Okay land owner," I said loudly. "If this is yours, forgive me."

I stepped off the sidewalk and took two steps to the base of the wall and from among the hundreds of tiny crumbs of rock I picked up a broken piece of black stone. It was, still is, about as big as my thumb.

It is right now next to my mouse pad. When I correct a word or a sentence or a chapter, I look at that stone and think, you are amazing. You are old enough to know what was going on before there were people or mouse pads or pitch and putt golfers walking over your back.

You have seen and survived many mistakes in your time, like putting up condos further down Cambie.

You have hung in through floods and fires, including at least one gigantic inferno from your mother, and you still look good and feel solid.

Long after global warming cools off again and the Canadian dollar goes up, you will still be hanging in there. How can I feel bad about making a mistake when I have something as strong and long-lasting within reach whenever I want it.

That is why I think the woman on the beach is stronger than me. She parted with some things that were part of her life. I would hate to give up my lava stone.

On the other hand, the stones really were not hers. She said that. She had just borrowed them for a while and she was returning them.

My lava stone is not mine. It belongs to the pile of other stones at the base of the wall. If I returned it, it would be where it should be, and someday I will. Meanwhile it has not complained and I still have many mistakes to get through.

The Lucky Moles

If you are a mole you would have hit the jackpot to be in Vancouver. The official policy of the Park Board would drive most gardeners, homeowners and farmers crazy. Sensible but heartless people use smoke and flooding and poisons and spring traps with cruel steel teeth to kill moles, but not in the city parks. Here, just let them be.

You can see their hills almost everywhere. Always brown, always a neat pile of crumbled earth and always near another one—and then near another one and another one and, you know what, the place is filled with molehills.

After I saw those hills appearing almost everywhere in parks a few years ago I longed to do a story about moles because I feel so sorry for them. I could not imagine a lifetime underground in the wet and soggy everything. No warmth, no getting in out of the damp and never seeing anything.

I am standing with cameraman Murray Titus on a sidewalk near some molehills. Murray is very patient. He would prefer being on his sailboat facing into the wind. Now he is looking at molehills to pay for his boat.

Moles are blind, which you probably knew but I didn't until I read about them.

Here's what I learned. They are rodents that long ago sought safety by digging tunnels. They apparently liked it down there so they stayed.

After uncountable generations of living mostly in the dark their eyes slowly disappeared. That is the truth of the old saying: use it or lose it.

They did develop extremely strong front paws with even more extremely sharp front claws. If you find one wandering around don't bring it home as a pet.

And they mostly live on worms, which are also blind. This is a case of the blind eating the blind. Sorry.

Some very interesting things: they build two hills for each tunnel, one at each end, but one of the hills is slightly higher than the other so that the difference in pressure draws air in through one and expels it out of the other.

Says one mole to the other, "Lovely breeze down here today, isn't it? Makes you want to take a deep breath and go hunting for worms."

And speaking of worms, moles can hear when one of the poor squiggling creatures digs too far and, whoops, falls into a tunnel. Off runs the mole and . . . gulp.

Except they don't gulp them all. They are smart and know there will come times when the worm supply will dry up, so the moles dig pantries into the sides of their tunnels and stuff the extra worms in there and then seal up the walls.

The worms are apparently so happy being snuggled up with other worms that most of them stay put. Some of them even make more worms. It's a worm farm.

The thought that makes me feel most sorry for the moles is that after a day of digging and eating and packing away the groceries wouldn't it be nice to curl up in a warm, dry bed and dream. They may dream, but they don't get the warm and the dry.

For all these reasons I wanted to do a story about them. Pictures are easy, thanks to the incredible internet. Tiny cameras let you watch them running through the tunnels and chomping on worms. Lots of naturalists have still pictures of their snouts and eyeless faces and their incredible claws.

But the end of the news is not a science show and I am no authority on anything. I need a reason to put the little I have learned about anything on the air. Simply, we need someone who cares.

"Hello," I say to a couple of women walking by the molehills next to the sidewalk where we have been standing for twenty minutes waiting for someone to pass. Not many people walk by molehills. "Do you know anything about moles?" I ask the women.

There is that tilted head again. Of all the questions in the world, one of them is probably thinking—questions about politics, the economy, crime, cooking, the weather—why is this idiot asking about moles?

"No," they both said.

The next is a man. "No," he said.

Then some teenage girls. "I can't hear you," one said. "Take out your earphones," I said.

"What?" she shouted.

"Moles!" I shouted.

"What?"

"Moles. Those things that live down there," I said pointing to the hills.

"I thought that was dog poo," she said. Then she put the earphones back in and as a group they left, walking together but each in her own world.

"There goes the next generation of leaders of the country," I said to Murray. I added, "I quit. We aren't going to find anyone who cares anything about moles."

"Just try one more," he said.

"No. We are wasting time that we could spend finding something else."

"Just one more."

That is what I like about him. He is a sailor who knows how to wait for a wind. That takes patience and faith.

No one was coming.

"Wait," he said.

Then someone was coming. Two someones, young and in love, because they were holding hands and arms and looking at each other and laughing and happy to be together. Love has its own way of walking.

"Excuse me," said I with no conviction. "We were wondering if you ever think about moles?"

The young woman looked astounded. She looked at the young man then back at me and laughed.

I figured right there that I would quit and study accounting.

"He *loves* moles," she said, pointing to the him in her life. "He studied them. He is always talking about them."

Then he said, "I used to dream of being a mole." Honestly, it is on the video disc and in the story.

"No?!" I said, meaning everything in that word.

"I love the way they can be so cozy down there." He looked at the molehills.

"Even in the rain?" I asked.

"They have thick fur. And in the summer it's cool and it's not so cold in the winter. Perfect."

Because of him and a sailor with a camera and the amazing internet full of pictures we had a story about something that most of us, including me, had never seen. Thank you.

The Stick

She was pushing a tricycle with a stick. That alone was good enough for a picture, maybe good enough to make the day.

One end of the stick was in her hand, the other was tucked below the seat of the tricycle, and sitting on the seat was a two-year-old boy trying to steer.

Two-year-olds can't steer, which made the picture so much better. The woman pushing, mother I presumed, was the engine of the trike, but not the driver. The motorless vehicle operator was going left, then right, then left off the sidewalk into the bushes.

Beautiful.

"Hello." The usual. "Tell us about the stick, please."

"They think this stick is wonderful," she said.

Then her older daughter, six or maybe seven, came back. She had been walking ahead as six or maybe sevens will do, which is the first step in stepping away.

It is amazing to me how we all follow the same path, even though none of us know it. We are all programmed to grow but as far as I can see we all think we are the first and only ones on this road.

"That stick is everything," said the six- or seven-year-old.

"What?" I asked.

"It's for fishing and rowing and throwing and bows and arrows."

That was more than I had hoped for. In fact, I hadn't hoped for anything except pushing.

"Anything else?" I asked, trying to push the envelope with the neat message inside.

"Drawing," she said.

Here was another example of how good ordinary things can be. From seeing a woman pushing a trike we now had most of the activities of humankind.

We got to the fishing dock of Trout Lake. The six-, maybe seven-year-old, took the stick.

"Look, I am fishing."

She hit the water several times, telling the fish that if they would like to be caught this would be the time.

Then she dragged the pole through the water.

"Catch anything?" I asked.

"Net yet, but I will."

She sounded like Reilly. I will tell you—once again—about him next. It is a shame if you don't know about him because Reilly was the most important part of my life. Even more than God, even though I think God sent Reilly to me. Yes, that is a pretty big endorsement.

Anyway, back to the six-, maybe seven-year-old.

"Sometimes we use it like a spear," she said.

Then she took the stick and threw it like a spear, and I am glad I wasn't standing in front. It only went a tiny distance, about the length of my arm, but that would be enough to poke me somewhere tender and I was glad I wasn't there.

"And then a bow and arrow," she said.

She held up the stick like a bow that wasn't bowed and pulled back an arrow that wasn't there. Then, *bing*, she let the arrow fly.

Then she said, "We use it to row a boat."

She put the stick back in the water and pulled it like an oar.

"You are going pretty fast," I said.

"And I can go faster."

Then she took the stick out of the water and ran over to the ground near the wooden dock.

"We can draw pictures with it."

She made a circle, then some zigzags, then another circle.

Picasso would have taken note and made a fortune from it.

The mother of the two told me it was bamboo from her backyard. They go through a stick a week.

"Some little kid is always walking away with it," she said.

A story about the stick that beat out all electronic games and made the imagination of a six-, maybe seven-year-old, burst into being. No one around that pond or anywhere on the planet was happier than me.

We said goodbye. There was nothing else I could have wanted. Except then the girl took the stick from her mother, stuck it behind the tricycle like her mother had been doing and began pushing her little brother.

Now there was nothing more I wanted, except for every kid to have a stick and play with it.

Reilly

I have put off telling you as long as possible. There are lots of new stories and they are important, but Reilly always comes up. Someone asks me my favourite story or the most important story or what do I like to talk about and it is Reilly. You know the story, right?

There is nothing new about it, except that every day when something bad happens or something good happens or something that I want to happen happens, there is Reilly again.

I was at Trout Lake. The cameraman, Dave McKay, and I were looking for something. There was a small kid fishing and he was wonderful from the start. His fishing pole was a stick with some leaves still attached. His line was hemp, so it was frayed, and when he pulled it out of the water we could see it had a safety pin for a hook.

And the bait was bread, squeezed by his fingers and barely holding onto the pin. Nothing, not anything Hollywood could create, could be better.

"Hello. Is your mother here? We'd like to talk to you."

He looked at us, then pointed off to the side of the lake and said with slow, measured, almost painful words, painful because they were so slow, "My foster mother is over there."

Foster parents have saved the world, or at least the world of many kids. Before them there were orphanages and in the orphanages kids without parents slept in barracks like in basic training in the army.

There was no privacy, no tucking in, no sweet goodnights. They woke to the commotion of dozens of others. The possibility of saying they wanted to stay in bed a few minutes more was not in their world. Saying they wanted anything was not in their world.

Foster parents changed that. They may not be a real parent but they are very close. The kids get a goodnight and in the morning a nudge, and that's not bad.

But when the boy with the fishing pole said his "foster mother" I knew he had had a hard life. You don't get a foster parent if things are going well. And when he spoke so slowly I knew he had had an even harder life. You don't talk like that and have many friends or go to a public school or have conversations. You answer questions and then go quiet.

His mother was in a portable chair reading a book. She had been watching us.

She said his name was Reilly and yes we could talk to him. She said he was quite wild but calmed down when he came to the lake.

Dave and I walked out on the short fishing deck and I kneeled down to talk. Dave stayed standing and pointed the camera down at an angle at Reilly.

"Caught anything yet?" I asked. It is the only question for someone fishing.

"No (pause) not yet," Reilly said. "But (pause) I (pause) believe."

If you find that hard to read, it is harder to listen to.

"I believe that (pause) if (pause) you believe . . ."

And right there is when he sucked back some mucus that was

149

dripping out of his nose. It went back up into his head with a slurp. It made my eyes open and my stomach tighten.

Then he continued without dropping a word or a pause, "you can (pause) do something (pause) you can (pause) do it."

So slow. So beautiful. So painful. So eloquent. So disgusting with the mucus. I didn't expect any of that.

"Have you had a nibble?"

"No . . . but I . . . believe . . . I . . . will."

That is easier to read.

But again the mucus, which was tinged with green, was slipping close to his upper lip before he again sucked it back up.

And then he continued.

"You can . . . do any . . . thing . . . if you . . ."

And again the sliding glob slipped down from his nose and again it got vacuumed up.

". . . believe . . . it."

Two things were going on at the fishing pier, and neither of them had anything to do with fishing.

1) I was listening to a Buddhist or Christian or Jewish or Muslim philosopher.

2) I was going to throw up.

I wanted to ask something else, but I couldn't get out any words without something else coming out of my mouth. I stood up and turned to Dave.

"Did you see that?"

"I saw everything," he said. "It was beautiful."

"Did you see his nose?"

Dave looked at me oddly.

"Nose?"

"Did you *see* the nose?"

"Are you nuts? What are you talking about?"

150

"Did you see what was coming out of his nose?"

Dave still looking at me in an uncomplimentary way. "No."

"You didn't see the runny nose?"

"No. I heard him sniff, but I didn't see anything."

Oh, wonderful! Oh, super wonderful!!

Because of where he was standing he couldn't see it. If he had been able to see it we would have had a story about a kid with a runny nose that probably wouldn't have passed the good taste censors in the edit room.

Because he didn't see that, we had a story of determination and positive thought and faith. Wonderful!

This gets better, but before we even left the park I realized much of life is like that. If something is bad just move slightly, either in your feet or your head, and you may see it entirely differently.

Such good advice I gave myself!

But the bigger thing, after the story was on the air, was that I started using Reilly's words. I didn't believe them but I had nothing to lose, and I needed all the help I could get.

What I needed was to find a story every day. I was pretty good at it but once in a while the day would get near the end, the sun was gone and I had nothing, which was bad.

Calling the office was worse. "Sorry, I have nothing."

A groan at the other end. Then I could hear, before the phone was hung up, "Find something to fill in for . . ." and then the phone was down. Clunk. The clunks hurt.

So, "I believe I will find a story." I didn't actually believe it but it was good to say it, just in case.

Then I said it again, and I didn't believe it again.

And there, around the corner, was just what I was looking for. How did that happen?

The next day I said it again. Okay, maybe now I believed it just a tiny bit but not really.

And around the corner, wow. How did that get there and why did we turn at that particular corner? I don't know.

And the next day. And the day after.

The days became weeks, as they always do, and then months and there were no fill-ins at the end of the show.

And then it became years. That amazed even me. Did just saying it trick some part of the back of my head into believing it? Did believing it make it happen?

I don't know, but the years became more years.

I know the self-help books all say the same thing, but who believes them?

And I know the Bible says sort of the same thing: you will get help if you help yourself, and you know a little help is all you need.

It has now been a decade. Sometimes an hour or two goes by, but then I say, out loud, "We will find something," and I look for a hole in the clouds and ask for a little help. Who the heck believes in holes in the clouds? But after that I believe we will find something.

And around the corner, well you know what is around the corner. And I say afterwards, "How the heck did that happen?"

It's free. Use it if you like.

I did the same thing with my health and I got healthier. Okay, I've had shingles and the flu and once a twisted bowel that almost killed me, but overall I've been healthy.

I also did the same with getting along with my wife. We are pretty happy together, but there are times. You know.

So I say things will be fine and then—no arguments. To be totally truthful, sometimes my wife has a problem with me, which means Reilly's method is only close to perfect, like me.

Again, if you have read this before I thank you for reading more than one book. And if you have read it you know it works. If you've read it and you haven't tried it, that's just plain silly.

As for Reilly, I got a call from someone after the story was on the air. He wanted to give Reilly a new fishing rod. I called the foster mother, she talked to Reilly and then came back to the phone.

"He says he will catch a fish with his own rod, and he believes that," she said.

I never saw him again. I assume they moved or he went to another home or he graduated to another goal, but I do know that somewhere, somehow he caught a fish.

John and Gerry

He laughs about his time in the war. It was ghastly, scarily terrible, but he laughs. In his eyes you can see the horror of it. He doesn't talk about it. His laughter covers it up.

That's Gerry MacPherson, and that is the kind of name that fought on one side in the Second World War.

John Schleimer is the kind of name that fought on the other side in the same war, but John doesn't talk much about it either, because he says, "You can't explain it. You just can't. You can't let anyone know how bad it was because . . ." And then he goes silent.

John laughs a lot, too. He laughs about fishing with politicians and hockey players. He got to know a lot of people because he was a barber for, well, forever in North Vancouver. Barbers know a lot.

But then he started talking about something no one could understand, not even him. He was in Hitler's army, conscripted when he was teenager. He didn't want to be but that had nothing to do with it. When he was seventeen he was captured by some of the fringe forces in Yugoslavia who were fighting the Germans.

John and I were having lunch when he told me that story. He put down his sandwich.

"Even when I was there I couldn't explain the fear to anyone.

"We were told to throw down our weapons. Then take off our uniforms. The soldiers turned us over to a gang of kids. They were twelve or maybe fourteen years old.

"They were wearing rags. They put on our uniforms and then started shooting in the air all around us with our rifles."

You cannot eat while you think of that.

It was long and hard. Excuse me for using those words but I have no others, just as he had none. What am I saying, of course, is that it was a long, hard road from the prison camp he was sent to through a destroyed Europe and through applying to move here to Canada. Those are cliché words, long and hard. It was unimaginable.

But he ended up in Vancouver and a year later brought his wife whom he had met after the war ended but before the cleanup was started.

She was walking to a village to hunt for her family. John saw her walking alone and he offered her a ride on the crossbar of his bicycle.

This was one of those old bicycles with a brake that was a piece of rubber that you could press on the front wheel by pulling up a lever on the handlebar. This was not like impressing a girl with your fancy car.

In North Vancouver they flourished with a family and happiness.

Back to Gerry, about whom I know much less. I only met him when a couple I have known for decades told me I should see a special garden. George and Freda Ellis took me there. They were bubbling about how amazing the garden was and how even more amazing the gardener was.

"You won't believe it," said Freda.

"Even better than that, we don't believe it," said George who makes a hobby out of meeting people and learning about them and then telling me, which makes him always fascinating to listen to.

I like hard-to-believe things, and I like special gardens.

It was beautiful, just like they said—flowers and a couple of gravel paths and a bench.

"Very nice," I said, but I didn't see what was special about it.

Then George took me a few steps past the garden into a mess of tangled blackberries and broken bushes and some garbage.

"That's what the whole area looked like before Gerry started cleaning it," he said.

It was amazing, truly beyond what you or I could believe. It was a transformation from uncontrolled disaster to comfortable beauty.

"And it is all on city land," George added.

Then he said, "You know why he did this?"

"He likes destroying his hands on the brambles?" was my wiseguy answer.

"His son died. Cancer. And Gerry did this in his memory," said George.

A lesson: don't ever give a flippant answer unless you know for sure it won't hurt someone, which is never.

A few days later I met Gerry. He came on a warm morning as he almost always does, to pull weeds and straighten flowers as all good gardeners do. He had started the garden when he was in his late eighties.

He was more than friendly. He was happy. He showed me a bench that had a plaque on it with his son's name. It was then that his face lost its joy, but just for a moment.

"It's all for him," Gerry said.

Because my friend George had told me about him I was there to put it on television.

Pete Cline, the cameraman, started to take pictures. He had flowers and Gerry, and then something truly amazing happened.

Into one of his shots, walking with his dog through the brush behind the garden was John the barber. He was surprised to see me. This was more than two years before we started occasionally meeting for lunch, and in truth I hadn't seen him for years.

He told me his wife had died a few months ago. They had been together sixty-three years and he was still in shock from losing her.

He had occasionally seen Gerry working on his garden and nodded but that was all. This time, because it was time, because we were there, he started talking to Gerry. They sat on the bench and the German ex-army soldier and the Canadian ex-army soldier who had been in the same war on opposite sides talked.

They each turned a bit to face one another and in doing so Gerry had his left elbow on the back of the bench and John had his right elbow on the back.

That left their hands so close they could have touched. Pete was taking video of the hands while the two ex-soldiers who had each lost someone so dear talked about things that we could not hear.

As they talked their hands made gestures. One went up, then fell down, then the other's hand did the same. It was a poem of silent conversation.

Much later the story was given an award by the news directors of British Columbia. That was nice but all we had done was watch two broken hearts in two strong men sharing pain. At the end we heard laughter and we saw their hands just for a second jump up at the same time.

I didn't know what they had said but sometimes laughter is as good as ducking under a bullet.

How did George meet Gerry?

"By accident. I was walking my dog on the trail and he was clearing the ground and we started talking."

Since then he and Freda have visited Gerry and his wife, Molly, many times. It's the way things happen, just by walking down a trail and saying hello. Imagine the stories we could all have if we just said hello.

And only because of that was I there on the day that John walked down that trail. And only because of that John and Gerry got to share things only they could understand.

All because George said hello to a fellow pulling up weeds—and none of this was planned.

The Smile

First we saw a woman sitting alone on a bench in the middle of the park. That was a sad but also lovely sight. It was lovely in the way that a photographer's image of a tree by itself can be, but a really good photographer would have something else in the picture, something that you can barely see but once you've seen it you can never not see it again.

I have a picture of a tree, alone, on my wall. There is nothing else in the picture except a vast, empty field. I paid more for the frame than the picture. I wish I had looked for a picture with something else in it.

And then I saw that the little old lady did have something else. She was smoking. Ugh! It is not my right to pass judgment on anyone but the cigarette didn't do much to raise the value of the picture.

Still, she might be wonderful. We would just wait until she finished the smoke.

"Hello."

Grunt.

"How are you?"

A quizzical look meaning, who the heck are you?

"Have a good day." And we left.

Next a woman on a cellphone. As we get closer she is arguing, loudly.

Following her comes a woman walking on the sidewalk of Comox Street, alongside the park. The park is wonderful. It is right behind St. Paul's Hospital, and Steve Saunders, the cameraman, suggested this park to find something interesting. Also, it was close to the television station and we had little time.

Many people who live in the West End walk through or alongside the park. Many of them are elderly and many elderly people are more patient than younger people. That is why I like them.

There is one coming this way. She has a shopping cart. She doesn't look happy but then again how many of us walk around with a smile? She is tiny and her cart is half her height and what more could I ask for? Steve takes her picture.

"Why are you taking my picture? Who gave you the right to do that? You better erase that picture or there will be trouble."

Not all older people are patient.

Then, like the sun breaking through the clouds, came the smile from far down the street. You could see it half a block away, all contagious happiness.

The woman carrying it was using a walker, one of those with wheels, and while she moved slowly along she was watching some kids who were playing while they were walking with their parents. Kids can make games out of putting one foot in front of the other.

Their mother had her face covered. The man did not. It is not mine to judge.

The kids started running circles around their parents. The woman with the smile almost laughed.

"Hello." That's us to the woman with the smile.

"Oh, hello. What can I do for you?" That was the smile speaking.

Anyone who asks that after the first hello is an angel, which is another way of saying smiles have pleasant ways of talking.

I told her we were looking for someone with a smile. She said she always smiled because life was so good.

She had just come from the Wesley United Church, a long block and a half away.

"I was with toddlers and their parents. There were more than forty of them. They were so noisy, but it was wonderful."

She kept talking. It was not a brief "I just came from church," or "I'm in a hurry to get home." It was an explanation of what she had been doing with a location and a punchline. Not bad for letting us know why she was smiling.

I asked her name. Margaret. I asked if she walked on this street often.

When you are young you go to a bar and ask a pretty young woman: "Do you come here often?" At the other end of life you ask a beautiful woman with a walker on a sidewalk the same question. The bar can lead to a good time. The sidewalk can lead to a good life.

"Every day for twenty years," she said. "I go to the church to volunteer. The last woman to do it quit when she was ninety. I'm eighty-five so I still have some time." She laughed at her joke.

Then she leaned forward and hid her mouth behind a mitten-covered hand and whispered, "I had a stroke, so I try to walk a lot."

There was no bitterness or even self-pity in her voice. She just had to get out and walk and that was that.

I thought, "Good for you." I didn't say it. I thought it would be condescending.

Then I asked why was she smiling when she was walking here?

"I feel good about life. No fooling. I think you can feel bad or good. The choice is yours. So I feel good."

So simple. So real.

Still trying to make something good for television, I asked, "Has anything incredible happened to you, or anything bad?" Then I quickly added, "I don't mean to pry and I hope nothing bad."

She smiled again and she tilted her head as I have seen many do when they have something to tell you that you might not believe.

"My husband died when he was thirty-seven. My oldest daughter was killed in a car crash. I raised three children on my own."

"Oh, I am so sorry."

"It's okay, that was a long time ago."

I have now added up one stroke, one dead husband and one dead daughter. Even in modern math that does not equal one smiling face.

"What's this?" I asked, looking down at her walker, which was carrying a large empty plastic container.

"I make cookies for the church. I bring them every Sunday and take back the empty box in the middle of the week. Then I make more. That's why I walk so much on this street."

"Thank you," I said.

"Did you get a scratch on your face?" I asked. There was a Band-Aid on her cheek near her nose.

"Skin cancer," she said.

"What?"

"Oh, it doesn't matter. I've had it since I was sixteen. A doctor used laser treatment to get rid of my acne and I've had skin cancer ever since. When the patches get big enough they cut them out."

Ouch. That means she has had skin cancer for sixty-nine years, and all that time wearing bandages on her face to cover it up and then having someone use a sharp piece of steel to take a slice out. Ouch again.

"There was a little girl in the church this morning. She pointed to my bandage. I said 'Grandma has an ouchie.' She said, 'I'm sorry. I hope it doesn't hurt too much.' She was three years old."

Then she said, "Isn't that wonderful. It just makes you happy."

Then Margaret said she was almost home. She pointed to the next apartment block on Bute Street.

"Goodbye," we said, and I watched her walk away. If you have a bad day, try thinking of Margaret. She never has one.

Horse and Cat

$\mathcal{T}$he important thing about this is you could do it yourself. You really don't need a television station or newspaper standing behind you. I know I keep saying that but that's because I mean it.

You can just go out and find stories on your own. No union problems, no layoffs and no scheduling problems. No bosses complaining you didn't get what they thought you would get, and you can take a coffee break whenever you want.

Be your own story-gathering enterprise and tell the stories to whomsoever you like. As for compensation, you get it in the thrill and excitement you give to others. No taxes on that.

It was raining, very hard.

"Can it get any harder than this?" asked cameraman Steve Murray. He's the same Steve who was getting the pictures of the balloons released for the teacher who was killed.

"You know the answer to that," I said.

We were driving around Stanley Park just in case we saw some people standing under a tree. That would be bad for them but good for us.

There were no people under a tree, but then I saw a group walking across the meadow near Lumberman's Arch, which is no longer a real arch. It once was. Look up the pictures on Google. It was something to be proud of. That was when the forests created most of the economy for the province. Now there is worry that the forest canopy in and around the city is so devastated it is in an urban hospice. Sad.

One idea is to plant trees on top of the high-rise condos. Just make sure they are trees that don't grow too big or have long roots or attract squirrels.

Anyway, the people by the arch, which they ignored as they passed by because it is now so forgettable, were walking one way and we were driving the other. Steve stopped and I scrambled out with my umbrella and tried to catch up with the walkers.

I tried. But then I thought, Don't be silly. They were far away and I would have to run along the path, which is okay except I have on a black jacket, black pants and black leather shoes and I am holding an umbrella over myself.

And no doubt I would meet a biker on his two-thousand-dollar racing machine with his skin-tight bicycle clothes and his form-fitting helmet who would shout at me, "You're going the wrong way, idiot."

And then I would have to say, "It's none of your business, fella."

And he would say, "You have to follow the rules," but by this time he would be so far away I wouldn't be sure what he was saying.

But in case he had said that I would have to shout, "You are riding in the jogging lane, so there."

You know how it goes. Someone honks, which is impolite, at someone else because they didn't turn fast enough at the traffic light and then the one getting honked at has to raise one of his hands and do something with one of his fingers, which is also impolite.

More honking and more fingers and before you know it you are hearing about it on the news because it has ended in some impolite way.

So I stopped chasing them.

Steve already had his camera out and I got back to him just as a horse-drawn wagon with three tourists was passing by.

I once saw a wagon with one passenger just at this same spot in the same kind of rain. The cameraman and I jumped on the wagon thinking we could do something nice with one person. Wrong. The person had nothing to say.

But as the horses clipped and clopped along, the driver with a leather cowboy hat that was dripping with rain began to sing. She was beautiful, her voice was beautiful and so were her songs.

She had written funny things about salmon and rain and Vancouver and the park and put them into the tunes of songs we knew. I've forgotten them now, but basically "Tennessee Waltz" was now "Fishing for Salmon" and "Singin' in the Rain" was "Crossing the Street in Vancouver." She was so good.

We listened and took pictures and had a wonderful story. We got off where the horse ride starts at the beginning of the park and asked when she would be going around again.

"Nope. That's the last for the day."

Our van was at the other side of the park where we had got on, and it was raining even harder. We had to walk back and believe it or not when we got there a half-hour later the battery in the van was dead. Things like that do happen.

We were saved by another camera truck that was not too far away. The story was good and we were wet and I think of it whenever I pass by that spot and a wagon and horses are passing by at the same time.

I said you can do any of this, and yes, you can, but unlike us, use your common sense.

You'd think we'd learn to keep an eye on the weather, but on this occasion several years later Steve was putting his camera back into the suv when the sky literally opened up. We weren't just standing in the rain, we were drowning. You know what it's like. You've been there. But we still had a story to get.

Go to the police horse barn, I suggested. It is dry.

Now here is where you actually could do the same thing. You could call them, ask to visit and believe it or not they will say yes. You can't get into the place where the undercover cops hang out, which is a scary place. I was in there once and even though I had been around police much of my life I could not believe what I saw in that room.

In there were the kind of seedy people you would send to prison without a trial just because you *knew* they were guilty. You can't go in there, but the mounted squad is different, especially if you want to bring kids.

We didn't make a phone call. I walked into the barn and saw Emily raking through the hay on the floor of a stall. Almost everyone loves horses but in every horse barn in the world there is someone who not only loves them but cleans up. That's Emily, in work clothes and a knitted hat.

"Anything new and wonderful and super?" I asked.

With her rake still in her hand she goes, "Shhhhh," and points to the seat inside her little manure-hauling, hay-hauling utility truck.

On the black seat is a black cat, sleeping. Of course it is sleeping. If a cat is not eating or playing or looking for food or looking for something or someone to play with it is sleeping. Cats are very smart.

"She's new," Emily said. "She got evicted from her last home and now lives here."

Nothing could be better than something new under a roof where it was not raining.

I talked to Constable Conrad VanDyk, who was getting ready for a ride in the storm. "I don't mind the rain," he said.

A good lesson: when you love your job you don't mind anything.

This next bit is a sidebar but it's important. Later that day on my way home I went for a haircut. I sat in the chair and the barber asked how my day was.

"Super," I said. "How's yours?"

"Passable," he said with a low, unenthusiastic voice. "When I get off work I'll be better."

Wow! If I had had the courage and the time I would have gotten up, excused myself politely and left, but having neither of those I sat and he cut. I felt sorry for him, spending all day doing something he didn't like. I felt sorry for myself, too, letting him do that thing that he didn't like on the top part of me.

I thought of Conrad, the cop on a horse, who loved what he was doing. You could see it in his face and feel it in his voice.

And I thought of Emily, who had the less regal job of shovelling stuff and feeding and grooming and she loved her job.

And I thought of John the barber from a few stories ago. He cut hair until he was eighty and if you asked him how his day was on any day he would smile and say, "Wonderful." John loved meeting people and talking about things that others liked. And he gave the best haircuts anywhere.

Sorry for the detour, but every journey has them. Now, back to the barn.

Princess the cat opened her eyes when Steve turned on his camera light to take a picture. Sorry to wake you, cat, but as I said, black cat, black seat, no light, no picture.

Being a cat, she just closed her eyes and rolled over, a very good lesson in life. If things don't look good one way, look somewhere else—unless you are looking at something bad that needs fixing, in which case you need to open your eyes, focus and fix it, unless you are a cat.

"We wanted a cat for the barn. We had mice," said Conrad.

Of course they had mice. There isn't a barn on earth that doesn't have mice.

"We sent in a requisition form. It went up through the channels and was rejected."

This is what I love about people in administration anywhere. In one way or another they are not going to allow a cat to do what poison or traps cannot do as effectively. If you don't think about that it makes sense. There is no column for a cat in the spreadsheet of any budget.

A cat can get rid of rodents easily and it doesn't miss any. Poison on the other hand leaves the little creatures in pain before they die an agonizing death of thirst. Then birds or other animals eat the dead mice and get sick and then other animals eat them and get sick. Brilliant idea.

As for traps, even the humane ones where the mice crawl in and can't get out still have to be emptied, and that's after the mice have spent a while in a state of panic at being trapped. The emptying part, which is done far away by someone else, still ends in unpleasant killing, and then the carcasses go into a landfill, which is always nice.

On the other hand a cat hunts the mice down, certainly causing a little panic before it kills, but not like a trap or poison, and then it eats them, eliminating the problem of what to do with the dead creatures and saving you bills for cat food.

So, again, it makes perfect sense for someone in a tenth-floor office with a carpet and a beautiful view of the city to deny getting a cat for a barn with doors that don't reach the ground—if you don't think about it.

Fortunately for the barn, the Park Board workers next door moved and couldn't take their cat with them. So the good police force on horseback took in Princess.

"Where was she before she was there?" I asked.

"Don't know. She just wandered into the park we guess."

"What about the superiors downtown?"

Conrad smiled, a big smile. Even though this was "technically" not approved, and he did the quote marks with his fingers around "technically," it was okay, he told us.

Of course it was okay. No one could approve something that was not approvable, but it had long proven to be the best solution for the problem.

Steve was taking another picture of Princess, but the horse in the stall behind him was curious and nudged the back of Steve's head, which made taking pictures difficult.

Then the horse did it again and I took out my phone and took a video of Steve getting nudged, which was much more fun to watch than a sleeping cat.

And then Emily got in the driver's seat of the little utility vehicle and drove out of the barn with a load of . . . stuff . . . in the back of the truck. Princess never moved from her curled-up rest on the seat next to her. No one in administration could find a problem with that.

March 3, 2016

Earlier in this book I talked about going to the Northwest Flower & Garden Show. When we came home my wife and I wanted to do something with our own garden straight away but it was dark and raining and the crows had ripped up the grass looking for grubs and it was late and I was tired. Three weeks later we are still waiting for spring, and when it arrives we will do something.

But today, March 3, 2016, is the twenty-fifth anniversary of the beating of Rodney King. I'm sure you remember him. What happened to him led to giant changes in the world of policing and criminals, especially black ones.

Rodney King had nothing much to put on a resume. He was involved with drugs and crime and generally bad stuff.

On March 3, 1991, he was stopped by the Los Angeles police for a traffic violation. He was not a good guy, and he looked drunk and possibly was on crack or plain old cocaine or some other drugs that made him uncontrollable and gave him extra strength. Before he could be given a traffic ticket he did some things that were perceived as offensive and in a defensive move a swarm of police descended on his defensively violent body and beat him with clubs and boots and fists.

It would have been just another day in LA, but there was a new invention being tested by someone nearby—a camcorder. This was before cellphones with cameras had been invented. The camcorder was a small video camera that used an even smaller video tape and it could do remarkable things, like record the beating of a drug-crazed driver by a gang of violence-crazed police.

It went viral before the word viral was used by anyone except scientists. It went everywhere and changed how people viewed police who were not being policed.

Similar scenes are still being shot and watched by millions almost weekly, certainly monthly, proving that the power of the media isn't great enough to have quick effects, but twenty-five years ago it affected someone: me.

I was so upset by seeing such uncontrolled nastiness that I had to do something. When I watched the beating on television I thought of some of the things I had seen in New York when I was a crime reporter.

I thought of police I had seen beating a black guy they had just cornered, ten against one. I thought of a gang of black teenagers that I saw on a street beating an old white man. I ran toward them but they fled before I got there. His face was battered and his pockets torn. They just wanted his wallet but they hurt him badly. I can't be certain, but I suspect he didn't live long after that.

And I thought of the prison guards after a riot had been put down, making the prisoners crawl the gauntlet of guards and bats. The guards were in two long lines, maybe fifteen in each. They all had police nightsticks, which were filled with lead, or baseball bats. The prisoners were made to walk between the lines of guards who slammed them on the backs and legs and heads with their sticks. When the prisoners fell they had to crawl along or lie there getting beaten more. If they were unconscious they were picked up and thrown outside the lines. The pile of unconscious prisoners grew higher and higher.

I watched this from a window in a factory overlooking the prison yard. The story I wrote about it resulted in a grand jury indicting twelve of the guards. The guards did not like me.

I also thought of old newsreel pictures I had seen of Nazis beating Jews.

It was not uplifting watching the news of Rodney King.

So I did the only thing I could think of doing. I went into my backyard, got a shovel and started digging.

Raking or hoeing or pulling up weeds wouldn't do it. The real violence I had seen needed something heavier to make it go away.

I dug and then dug some more. I drove the point of the shovel into the ground with all the bitterness and strength I had, just trying to get over the endless pain that we as people put us as people through.

The dirt went flying up over my shoulder and the thoughts of nastiness went through my head. I got tired and then I dug some more.

In a while, and I don't know how long it was, I was in a hole up to my chest. The anger was not going away but on the other hand I felt proud that I had done something significant, even if it was just digging a hole.

Then I thought, "How do I get out?" The sides were sloped and the soil was now more mud than dirt and my leg wouldn't go up that far and when I tried putting my hands on the surface all I managed to do was drag my shirt and pants over the slush.

This is not good, I thought, but at least I was no longer thinking so much about bad things. On the other hand I was in somewhat of a bad situation. Okay, it wasn't a serious bad situation but it was pretty stupid bad.

If my wife came home and looked out the back door she would say, "Why are you in a hole?" That would be an understandable thing to ask.

And I would say, "I felt like digging a hole."

And she would say, "I can't hear you."

That was because I didn't want to say it loud enough for the neighbours to hear. I would say just a tiny bit louder: "I felt like digging a hole."

And she would say, "I still can't hear you but why are you in a hole?"

I wouldn't want to shout, "Because of Rodney King!" because she probably wouldn't have heard the news and I really didn't want the neighbours to hear me shouting about someone they might not have heard of while I was down in a hole.

If I was still in the hole when she came home I wouldn't be able to ask her to help pull me out because I knew the first thing she would say would be, "Your clothes are filthy. You shouldn't have done that," and I would think she was missing the entire point of the social injustice I was trying to overcome.

Right after that she would add, "You should get out of that hole and take off your clothes but don't put them into the machine because it will ruin it. Just hose them off. But don't take them off in the backyard because the neighbours will see you."

I could imagine it all: "Go into the garage, but don't go too far because you'll track mud inside and I'll have to clean it up. But just go near the door and take off your clothes. I'll bring you something to put on. But try not to get them dirty."

So you can see why I had to get out of the hole, quickly.

I came up with a plan. I would stick the shovel in the bottom of the hole, use it as a pole, push myself up so I could put my hand on the ground, then dig my knees into the muddy side of the hole and push and pull my way out.

Didn't work.

I had a better idea. I picked up the shovel and started digging away at the edge of the top of the hole, putting the dirt in the bottom of the hole. Brilliant. I could stand on the dirt and reach the trench I was creating.

Not so brilliant. I was undoing the greatness of the hole. How could I brag about the size of a hole I had dug to overcome a bad feeling if the top was lower and the bottom was higher?

You probably know guys are basically nuts. We have things to prove, like running for president, winning wars or digging holes. And here I was turning my giant feat into half-hearted, wimpish semi-defeat.

On the other hand, my idea was working. The more I dug the trench at the top the more dirt was going in the bottom, which got me closer to the top.

I climbed out. No, truly I crawled out. The hole was wrecked. It was no longer the greatest hole I had ever dug. I was filthy and I hadn't changed anything in the world. I felt just as bad about the news but most of the anger was gone, and I had learned a universal truth. You can't be angry and exhausted at the same time.

However, the next time I was very upset about something I would put on a pair of sneakers and run around a track until I couldn't run any farther. No anger, no dirty clothes and my wife would be happy thinking I was exercising.

Luckily for me I haven't gotten that angry again since then.

Unluckily for me my wife keeps wanting me to take up running.

The Next Day

Now I had a hole in the backyard and it was difficult to explain to my wife. It wasn't even a good hole. One side was lower than the other.

"Why?" I was asked.

"A fish pond," I said. "I've always wanted a fish pond."

"No you haven't," my wife said.

"Yes I did; I just didn't tell you," I said.

"Well I hope you do something because it doesn't look good."

I read about fish ponds. This would be a lot of work and I did not want to do a lot of work, I just wanted a fish pond.

That is another universal truth. Between the desire and the having of what you desire there is time and space. There is also sweat, worry, money, scratched fingers, elation and despair.

This was one of Einstein's unwritten theories: getting what you want is directly related to how much time and space you have in your garage or workshop or life to devote to it. If he had written it on his blackboard it would have been wwmis, or Wishing Won't Make It So. I know you have heard of that.

The formula takes a lifetime to work out and usually at the end of it you have run out of time, or if you do finish it you don't have the space to display it.

"You are *not* putting *that* in our living room."

All of the above goes into making a fish pond. Warning: don't try it unless you have a lot of time and space, and the ability to accept failure.

I have written about this before but in case you missed it here it is again. If you do know the story, no you can't get back your money, but you can skip to the end where there is something new.

A friend gave me a rubber tarp that had come out of another fish pond. She also gave me an old pump. I didn't know that to make a natural pond nature needed help.

I'm ready to put in the tarp, but wait! You must protect the tarp from stones and roots so first you have to line the hole with newspapers. I only read one paper a day. This will take a lot of days.

Early the next garbage day, in the rain, I walked up our street going through the recycle bags of my neighbours. This included many, nay most, of the neighbours I did not know, but I do know that many of them looked out their windows and saw me going through their garbage. I also know this was followed by many of them making phone calls to others with this news.

News is a very exciting thing to hear, especially when someone who is somewhat, in a small way, known because he is occasionally on television is seen garbage picking

There are still people who talk about this to their friends. A few times I have had to explain it but to all the rest they have their story, and their story is better than real life.

This is another life lesson. The *National Enquirer* makes a lot of money with stories that are shocking to read. I like to read them, too.

My mother-in-law loves the paper, but the stories would be dull if the whole story was told, so don't tell it.

There were many *National Enquirers* in the papers that I picked up and then used to line the mud walls of the hole. On top of them went the tarp, just like those who slip the *Enquirer* inside the *Province*. No one will ever know.

Regarding the tarp, have you ever gotten frustrated trying to straighten a large bed sheet? Don't try to arrange a tarp in a hole.

Then I filled in the dug-out part of the top of the hole with rocks. Wait, that looks dumb. One part of the rim of the pond has rocks, the rest doesn't. Where do I get more rocks?

Many construction sites and many scratched fingers later, more rocks. Remember Einstein's unwritten theory about Wishing?

Then, after running a garden hose in the hole for a long, long time, the project was finished—or just beginning.

The next day, once the chlorine had evaporated, I went straight to the pet store.

"Would you like these koi? They're twenty dollars."

"For all of them?"

I left with twenty feeder fish, poor things that are born to die in the mouths of other fish. I would save them.

After I'd put the plants—which cost far more than the fish—in the pond, in went the fish. I was so happy. It started as a project to relieve pain and now it was bringing pleasure.

I watched the fish. Actually, I couldn't see the fish because they went straight to the bottom of the pond, but I pretended I could see them. Then I went to bed and dreamed of the fish.

The raccoons, it would seem, had no trouble seeing the fish. When I rushed out in excitement the next morning there was major destruction, nasty devastation and a real mess. The raccoons had rolled the rocks in the pond, pulled up the plants and somehow not missed a single fish.

If you know the story I'll get to the end quickly. I put a chicken wire fence around the pond and bought more fish and more plants. The raccoons went under the fence.

I hammered the bottom of the fence down with tent pegs, bought more fish and plants. The raccoons went over the top of the wire.

I put wire fencing across the top, bought more sacrificial living things, and the raccoons ripped apart the wire.

I put a second layer of wire everywhere. More fish. More plants. It was war and the raccoons were eating their way to victory.

One last stand. I put in more fish and promised them they would be okay. I think I heard them praying. Then I put plywood between the layers of wire on the sides and over the top.

I win! Except I couldn't see the fish or stones or plants or water.

"That's worse than the hole," my wife said.

And that of course meant something much deeper than just those words. I took it all down, the fish were given away, the hole was filled in and zucchini were planted, but the story has a new ending. Actually this was in the free book I gave away last Christmas, but forgive me.

I got two fish and a bowl for my granddaughters. They could see the fish. They were happy, and there is nothing better than that.

Behind the Art Gallery

It is such a simple instrument, sort of. Played by those who do it well a harmonica is like an orchestra played by gremlin musicians hiding behind the lips. Sometimes they are moody, sometimes touching. Sometimes they dance and move as fast as a Maritime fiddle.

I met and have gotten to know the fellow who plays a harmonica behind the art gallery. His name is Tim and he creates a microscopic symphony for the passing audience on the sidewalk.

He makes his living from his harmonica and a doll that dances to it. With one hand he gives life to his little performer and with the other holds his music machine.

And when someone passes by, which is almost constantly, he pauses the music and says, "Good morning," or "Good afternoon, mate," or "You're looking good today." Tim is a joy.

He carves his little people from pieces of driftwood. Their arms and legs are held to the body by wire. He showed me how he bores a hole through the end of a sliver of wood and then threads the wire through another hole in the body. A twist of the wire and the arm comes to life. More wood, more wire and you have both arms and legs—and feet. It is extra work but you can't forget the feet.

Add a head, of course, with a smiling face from a felt pen, and presto, a dancer is born. He squeezes a stick into a hole in the back of his new friend and with that in his left hand the dancer takes to the stage, which is a slab of wood resting on a cardboard box.

If there were a curtain it would be coming up.

"Hush."

That's me thinking. The street noise never quiets but I want to say "Quiet" because the orchestra is about to begin.

First of all, "Good day to you." Then the song, the symphony, the music of the street. His harmonica is as much alive as his dancer clicking on the board.

He has his begging box on the ground. Some days he makes ten dollars, some days twenty. Some days, bad ones, it is raining and folks are in a hurry. He never asks. He just plays and his little people dance.

And all the while he stops to say, "Good day."

Now walk cross the street, Hornby Street at Robson, and there is another man. He is kneeling on the ground on a piece of cardboard. He is so close to the crosswalk you have to walk around him.

He is about to begin his pitch. It is not a song, it is not music. It is a whine backed with aggression and anger.

"I hope you enjoyed your breakfast. I didn't have any." The sarcasm is nasty.

"Don't you see me? I'm hungry. You have money to buy food. I don't."

He has a line for each time of the day. In an hour he will be saying, "I hope you like your lunch. I didn't have any. I'm hungry. Go ahead, pass me by like I don't exist. What do you care?"

Most pass by because he has been there every day, except when it rains, for the three years I have worked downtown.

"Doesn't anyone see me? I'm hungry. You just ate and I'm hungry. What kind of people are you?"

The tourists give him money and get an impression of the city. The ESL students who have just learned the words "money" and "hungry" sometimes give him money. And the little old ladies who come to meet their friends because they haven't been to Robson Street for years give him money. They open their purses and take out whatever is in there.

After that they are sad. I can see their faces. I can hear their voices. Their day on Robson Street has had a bad beginning.

A few weeks ago I thought he was sick. He was bending over the newspaper boxes on the corner. But, no, he was talking on his cellphone and trying to hide it.

There is nothing wrong with a beggar having a cellphone. It is none of my business, and anyone who can afford one is entitled to have it. Tim with his dancing dolls and harmonica doesn't have one.

Tim was sick a few weeks ago. "I had something bad in my chest. Hurt. So I checked myself into the Sally Ann. They take care of me."

Then he added, of course with a smile, "I sang for my supper every night."

Last week, at 9:45 a.m. on Sunday, I saw the complaining one coming up from the SkyTrain station at Burrard Street. He walked half a block and then set himself down on his knees across the street from Christ Church Cathedral. He was just in time for the ten a.m. service.

"Doesn't anyone care about me? I'm hungry. You had breakfast. I didn't." He looks the churchgoers in the face and adds, "You are going to church and you don't even see me."

Many give. He does very well. I can only guess after watching on and off for three years that he makes well over a hundred dollars a day—tax free. That is for a four-hour day. Not bad if you can do it, and I have no argument with his act.

The only problem I have is with his whining, which doesn't add anything good to the day. It is like the person with the loud muffler who takes over whatever space he is in and pollutes it for most others.

And then the hungry man, who, like me, has gained a few pounds since I first saw him, takes the train home.

Across the street, just at sunset when I was downtown late, at the end of ten hours of playing and dancing and smiling, I saw Tim pack up his dancing dolls and his box and start walking home to Stanley Park where he has lived for the past four years.

My only point: if you are at Robson Square give Tim a dollar. Then have a good day for yourself. He will have earned it and you will deserve it.

PS: I've gotten to like Tim. He's always there, always filling the day with his music and his dolls. On St. Patrick's Day I was passing him when a young woman give him a tiny bouquet of tulips. So nice.

"Come back," I shouted.

She did. "Are you giving these for St. Patrick's Day?"

"No," the Chinese woman replied. "Someone gave them to me for a charity and I don't want them and I want to give them to someone else." That is very kind.

"Beautiful," I said because I liked the kind answer.

"Now would you do something else for us?"

Before she could say "No," or "I am in a hurry," I said, "Sing 'When Irish Eyes Are Smiling.'"

She looked at me blankly. Now she was frightened. This was a test and she did not have the answer.

"I don't know it," she said.

"Tim will teach you," I said, and he did. That was worth five dollars.

Survivor

I hate to tell you this. I hate to admit it. I am on the edge of not telling you.

Okay . . . fifteen minutes have gone by between writing the "you" in the last sentence and the "okay" at the beginning of this one.

How can I admit I watch *Survivor*? I mean, "Get real," and "Really?" and "You're kidding me!" and "Oh, I used to watch it, five years ago, or was it ten?" or very simply, "That old thing? Can't you get onto something new?"

Maybe I will retract the last fifteen minutes and not admit it.

In truth, it's more my wife who watches *Survivor*, not me. I think it is nutty and repetitive and silly.

Sure, some people have trouble making a fire and, sure, the girls are young and beautiful and wear skimpy bathing suits, and the guys are young and have big muscles and I hate them.

And sure, there is one old guy or woman in each group and he/she is held onto long enough to keep some government agency from complaining about age discrimination.

Then they get voted off.

And of course the girls wearing bikinis, who I do not look at, ever, have parts of the television picture blurred out when their bikinis fall off, which happens in most of their challenges.

For heaven's sake, of course I don't watch that. I am watching this with my wife and when the blurred-out parts come on she can look at me and see me looking at the ceiling.

It all started a few years ago when we were with a group of friends and the subject of *Survivor* came up.

I said, "My wife loves it." I was trying to add some inclusiveness to the talk.

Immediately someone else said, "Why doesn't she join our group? We watch it every week."

I have to admit that most places my wife goes, outside of her flower club, I go, and I am happy with that, but at home when she watched *Survivor* I stayed in another room. This was a good time to polish my shoes, or clean my desk, or think deep thoughts.

I would spend an hour trying to decide what to do, and when the show was over and my wife came back and asked what did I do with my time I would tell her I'd been thinking of polishing my shoes or cleaning my desk.

"And did you?" she would ask.

"No, I was thinking of it."

"You would not survive on *Survivor*," she would say.

I didn't tell her about the deep thoughts. I'm told that with deep thoughts you can survive anything. I just haven't had any yet.

Then this group invited my wife to join them and not to my surprise I went with her.

The group consists of the guinea-pig people whom I told you about earlier, Ingrid and Bob. Their guinea pigs run free, so while you watch people in the show trying to force themselves to eat rats you have little furry creatures scooting between your feet.

Then there is Julia who has rabbits in her apartment. They hop around, also free. They are trained to do what they do only on the part of the floor that's covered with something on which they can safely and cleanly do it—which is good.

On the *Survivor* show they have never killed and eaten a rabbit. The contestants have eaten many life forms that humans would not normally eat without the prospect of winning a million dollars, but when it comes to rabbits, the producers know there is a line that they cannot cross. That is a good thing because Julia would throw her television out the window if a rabbit was hurt, and that would be very bad because she lives twelve stories up.

There is Nancy who is Native and lives on the Capilano Reserve. She has a dog and a cat that live in peace and harmony, unlike many humans and entirely unlike what happens on the show where everyone is backstabbing everyone else. Nancy's dog and cat bring peace to the gathering.

There is Rosi who, like Julia, lives in a rented top-floor apartment. Both of them have views of the city and mountains that no one in the rest of the group has, even though they all live in houses. A view such as Julia and Rosi have could not be bought for any money, not even what is being paid by those who put down ten million dollars cash for a fixer-upper.

Rosi has a special needs daughter. I only tell you that because special needs children create special parents, especially mothers.

There is Leslie who also has a special needs son. He has severe problems and she has spent much of her life caring for him. She has never not been smiling or cheerful, and she always starts washing dishes before anyone else.

There are Kathy and Cam, who are in love. He is recently retired, so while it is young love, in his case it is young love in a body that is topped with white hair. As for Kathy she has said she never thought this could happen again at her age. It did happen. They have a cat.

And lately there is Kathy's brother Alan who, like a few others in the group, no names, is in his seventies. He just moved back to British Columbia from New Mexico, where he lived for decades. He has two pugs that have separation anxiety problems when they aren't close to him.

And there was Tanya who dropped out this year because she needs all her time to search for a job and a house and a new life. A year ago she took maternity leave when she got a new puppy.

Of course she didn't really get maternity leave for a dog but she took off time from her job, vacation time, to bond with it. She called it maternity leave and because of that she made the front pages of the life sections of newspapers across the country.

Where on earth would I find such a group as this? Each week they ... we ... meet in one house or another for dinner and then the show. The dinners are fantastic, usually with everyone putting out the best of something to eat.

Then the show. Over the years I've been told by those who watch that the plot has changed from actually trying to survive on raw bugs and a handful of rice to something everyone can associate with— cunning, lying and nastiness.

The contestants no longer lose much weight or wear the same clothes for more than a month. Now they simply get healthy by being outdoors and moving their bodies. They often show up with freshly pressed pants and dry-cleaned dresses. The days of rags and hunger are over.

Now it is a continuous case of "I will be on your side if we vote off that person and gang up on the other one before they undercut us."

And that is followed by the one who has promised to be on the side of the other one secretly plotting the demise of the first schemer.

The producers have figured out that starving is not as good for ratings as cheating. Watching someone sharing rice is not as compelling as watching someone stealing it, and seeing who can stand the longest on a thin board while holding plates on their head is not as good as listening to whispers between two enemies about how to chop off the knees of their friends.

This is reality. This is real ugly life in the comfort of your home without having a fight with someone in your family. This is what gives birth to gossip and sells the *National Enquirer* and starts wars and keeps the US Republican Party going. This is worth giving up part of your life for every week.

There is a lot more whispering and a lot more captioning in the show now. We don't want to miss the poison in the secret talks, so now we can read it. The producers leave the captions on extra-long for those who have trouble doing two things at a time, reading and thinking.

The only problem with all this is that the folks in this *Survivor* group talk, *while the show is on*, because they each have their favourites and they think they know what is going to happen. It is like going to a children's panto at Christmas.

"No, beautiful girl in the tiny bikini, they are plotting against you! Can't you see that?"

And of course she can't see it because she is the bimbo who can see nothing, but she will be among those at the end who are closest to winning the million dollars.

"See, told you," someone says to everyone. "The one with the tattoos over his back and sides and front and neck and arms and face is a nice guy."

Because of this I record the show myself and when we get home I have to watch it again because, except for the captions, I missed most of what happened because of the talk.

The problem with that is, I know you've guessed it, I don't have time to clean my desk or polish my shoes—but I do have some deep thoughts. I'm just saving them to see if the bimbo is smarter than me.

Later, one of Alan's dogs died, put down—cancer of course. Rotten, sad, all the heartbreak that goes with that. Ingrid wrote him such a nice note.

I could not imagine guinea pigs doing much grieving, but apparently I was wrong. She said when one of her pigs stops living she lays it on a soft blanket near the other pigs. They take turns, two at a time, one on each side, lying next to it, sometimes for half an hour.

A few weeks later Alan brought his other dog with him to *Survivor* night. Almost everyone took turns petting it.

Tulips and the Lady

What if, instead of finishing dinner, putting out the garbage, washing the dishes, opening a beer and sitting in front of the television to let someone else have an adventure for you with guns and arrests and kung fu—or, more recently, buying or selling a house—what if you said, "No"?

What if you said, "Let's do something wild. Let's go for a walk." Imagine what could happen. You could meet someone walking a dog and say, "Hello."

Someone I know did something like this a while ago. "Hello," he said to a woman planting tulip bulbs. He knew they were tulips. He doesn't know much about flowers but they were fat bulbs and so he felt they were tulips, and he took a chance.

You probably know about the great tulip investment war of long ago. You don't? Sorry. Detour.

In the mid-1500s tulip bulbs were brought to Europe from Turkey, and they created quite a stir. No one had ever seen anything like the flower that came out of them. By the early 1600s, Holland, which is now part of the Netherlands, had become a centre for their cultivation, and ever more wonderful, rare and multicoloured blooms were being created.

They were quite amazing flowers—beautiful, tender and . . . "This must be worth a fortune." Always money gets into the excitement.

Someone said the word "fortune," and by golly he was right.

When you have something that no one else has and you promote it as the best thing ever, you can sell it at whatever you want to sell it for. Soon they became a status symbol for the rich and famous, tulip mania took hold and almost overnight the price of tulips was like gold, or like oil when oil was the price of gold. Everyone wanted to invest in tulips because there was a fortune to be made. Sure they looked nice, but mostly it was "if we do that we can get rich."

And some did. You have heard of Ponzi schemes and pyramid schemes. Don't worry if you don't understand them; they are based on madness and greed. Tulips were sort of like that, only different in one important way. They are pretty. Beauty surrounded by madness and greed. Folks sold their homes to buy a tulip bulb. One brown onion-looking thing that would turn into a flower that would last two or three weeks was going for a year's salary, then two years', then more. Crazy. Like all crazy schemes.

Then someone said the obvious: "This is crazy. I'm not buying."

And the tulip bubble burst, with petals falling on terrified heads—like condos or oil or other madness.

Now the Netherlands has turned tulips into an industry, a hard-earned beautiful product that makes the world better and gives a decent living to many.

You can buy a bag of bulbs for an hour's worth of work, the way it should be.

I know you know all this, but thanks for listening.

"Planting tulips?" my friend said to the woman.

"Yes," she said.

People don't often jump into conversations with strangers.

"They will look pretty," he said.

"Yes," she said.

"Nice day for this," he said, just pushing it a bit. He sensed she wanted to be alone but what the heck. Being annoying to a tulip planter is allowed.

"I bet you look forward to seeing them," he said.

"I won't see them," she said.

"Moving?" he asked stupidly.

"No, dying."

Oh, my gosh. Oh no. Where has this gone? He hoped he hadn't caused hurt. He probably had. And, more importantly, what does he say now?

"I'm so sorry," he said.

"It's okay. I'm getting used to it."

"May I ask? Why . . . ? What . . . ?"

"Cancer."

When he told me what she said I was hurting. His hurt was worse, hers even greater.

"So why are you planting the bulbs?"

"So my neighbours can see the flowers after I'm gone. I like my neighbours."

I know you have felt tears filling your eyes at some time in your life and there was nothing you could do to stop them. And then the tears went down your cheeks. Well my hand went to my face, and I was only listening.

"That's nice," was all he could say.

I took a deep breath. He told me he did the same, and then said to her, "Thank you."

He walked away, but part of him stayed there—and is still there, along with a part of me.

Go for a walk. Talk to someone doing something. You never know.

Vimy Ridge

For once the generals got it right.

"By Jove, it will work," said one of them. Maybe he said it like that, because that is the way they talked in 1917, especially when Canadians were trying to sound British.

"It is so simple it will catch them off guard, ha, ha," another probably said.

"But if it fails we will be damned for not having a more complex plan."

Most of them said that, for sure.

The idea was a child's game: leapfrog.

"We will have the first trench attack. Damn the machine guns," said the idea man. "Then, before the Huns can recover, we will have our next trench leapfrog over the first trench and attack."

He slapped the side of his leg with his riding crop, or at least I imagine he did. If you are going to be a general in the first totally Canadian force you would have to act positively British. Slap away.

"And then the men from the first trench would leapfrog over the men from the second trench."

And again, "Damn the machine guns."

Ninety-nine years later to the exact same day, Alvin is picking up litter, which is really garbage, under the decorative helmets in Victory Square.

"Hate to bother you, but what'cha doing?"

"It looks so bad," he said. "This is an important place."

That was good enough for me to believe there was hope, even here. Victory Square has two main groups of citizens. The trendy office workers who bring their tiny dogs to work with them in baskets and at lunch time take them for a poop walk around the Cenotaph. (Yes, they pick up afterwards.)

And the drug dealers who skateboard and sit and lounge and smoke and push each other all day long, even on the anniversary of the men who leapfrogged.

The drugs got so bad a few years ago that the Park Board pulled out the shrubbery that grew throughout the park. The low shrubs were pretty but the dealers hid their stashes under them and occasionally they would steal from each other.

Only war is more violent than one drug dealer stealing the stash of another. And the violence was immediate and the location was all around the shrubs.

The Cenotaph is at one end of the park, the shrubs at the other, so the dog walkers and their little hairy friends were not in peril as long as they pooped quickly.

But what to do about the fighting at the other side of the park? Eliminate the drug dealers or eliminate the shrubs? The choice is easy. No more shrubs in the park. That is the park that on one day every year in November is sacred, so we have a sacred park with no shrubs. Nice, if you like it.

As a side note, the totally beautiful Dr. Sun Yat-Sen Classical Chinese Garden in Chinatown had the same problem. Half the garden is free for the beauty-loving folks who would stop by for mental, visual and emotional peace, and free for the drug dealers who would hide their day's inventory under the bushes.

The result there has been the same—no more bushes. You hardly miss them, like you hardly miss anything after a while, even if it was calming and beautiful.

Sorry; back to Victory Square. I apologize for going back and forth like a ping-pong ball, but stories are like that. Life is like that. Think of one thing and immediately you are thinking of something else and you forget the first thing. Crazy.

Victory Square.

"What's your name?"

"Alvin," said the man picking up the garbage. "I've got to tell you before you talk to me that I'm an alcoholic and I've been on welfare all my life so whatever I say doesn't matter."

I wish politicians were so honest.

"Why are you doing this?" I asked.

"This is an important place," he said again, and he looked at the Cenotaph. "Many people were killed here."

I said, "Not actually here."

He looked confused.

"They were killed in a war, a couple of wars, in Europe."

He nodded like he knew what I was talking about.

"Vimy Ridge?" I said.

Blank stare. Slow head shake.

"Lots of Canadians were killed on this day, a long time ago."

Then that look from Alvin like he wanted to know more. What kind of look is that? You see it in kids when you tell them something about themselves.

"Thousands of Canadians were killed on this day."

Alvin understood that. He nodded. He looked at the Cenotaph.

"That's what that is for?"

I nodded. "And other wars."

"I better get back to work," he said.

He walked off searching for more garbage. We watched him pick up a syringe, a used needle and a plastic tube that had sent someone to heaven and then hell. Without plastic gloves—of course you knew that, I knew that, but it is important to say it again—without the plastic gloves that are mandatory for anyone giving any help to anyone now, he picked up the syringe and broke the needle in half. One end of it flew off and landed on the grass. Alvin picked it up and put it into the plastic bag he was carrying.

Ninety-nine years ago Canadian soldiers with razor-sharp knives at the ends of their rifles jumped into the trenches where German soldiers with razor-sharp knives at the ends of their rifles were waiting. There was stabbing and screaming and when the fighting ended 3,598 Canadians had stopped breathing.

Seven thousand more had holes in their stomachs or had lost legs or arms or parts of their minds.

An unknown number of Germans were face-down or face-up or broken in half in the mud of the trenches. Four thousand were prisoners.

"It worked," said the general. "By Jove we will get a medal for this."

In wonderful truth, four Victoria Crosses were given to soldiers who played the child's game of leapfrog. They played it very well.

The last I saw of Alvin he was standing near the towering Cenotaph and looking up. He held his garbage bag in his hand. He was standing very straight, almost at attention.

The Little Lost Deer

OMG. Oh my gosh!

    We will only say it in a polite way. Oh my double gosh.

"There it goes."

"Where?"

"There, but it's gone now."

The "Oh my gosh" was the deer that had somehow gotten into Stanley Park. The where was anywhere in the park where it had been and now was not.

For more than a week this deer had been spotted by some but photographed by almost none. It popped in and out of sight too fast to get your phone out of texting mode and into camera status.

Actually, since you were texting your friend to tell her/him that you were in the park and you could meet her/him for lunch in twenty minutes as soon as you could get out of the park because it was boring and there was nothing to do here, you didn't see the deer at all. The friend you were with who wasn't texting shouted, "There's a

198

deer," and hit your arm, making you mess up the message you were writing and that got you annoyed.

Instead of saying, "What deer?!" with excitement you said, "You ruined my text!!" with a loud voice that the deer heard, causing it to run into the woods. It was then that you said, "What deer?"

Texting and wildlife are a disastrous combination.

Nonetheless, there was a deer in the woods that were once a forest that had many deer and beavers and a few bears and an occasional cougar and was surrounded on its edges by oysters and many fish.

Now there was one deer that had arrived there by accident—swimming, walking, maybe dropped off by an angel who wanted to see what would happen to a deer in the woods.

It made the front page of a newspaper. That was a lucky shot by a good photographer. Stories of it were on the radio. That was easy to do.

Then Jim Fong said, "There's the deer."

I wasn't texting. I was just looking in the other direction.

"Where?"

But before he could answer he had already pulled over, jumped out, opened the back of the SUV, taken out his camera and was running back across the street. I guessed it was there.

He managed to get two shots of the deer: one of its back end far away and the other of its back end even farther away.

"Nice," I said. "Very good. Now let's find something we can put on television."

Face it, you can't just use the back end of a deer and hope to keep your job.

We circled, and after extensive hunting found . . . nothing. That is so typical. It happens to me, you, us, them, and even those over there all the time.

The thing is that all the positive-thinking books in the world and all the idiotic, pandering do-gooder slogans that say "Never Give Up" are ridiculous. To think that if you keep banging your head against the wall the wall will fall down is a big "No." It doesn't happen. Who would honestly believe that?

That's what I think sometimes, despite Reilly. (You did read about Reilly, right?)

We found nothing. "Let's go to Third Beach, again," I said, in desperation. At least they have a toilet, and I have an ever-present need. And the sun came out, of course, as I knew it would.

Third Beach is my favourite spot. That is after Trout Lake and the Lynn Canyon Suspension Bridge, which may not be as long as the Capilano Suspension Bridge but it's free. If you have visitors, take them to the Lynn Canyon bridge. They will be amazed and not broke.

Anyway, at Third Beach there is Tom the lifeguard. He is big and handsome, as lifeguards go, and strong and friendly.

He is also one other thing. He has been doing this job longer than anyone else and is not only still ready, willing and more than able to run into the water to save someone's life, but he is not afraid of bureaucracy. Idiotic bureaucracy.

Let me just take a little diversion. For many, many years I have been doing stories about the parks and beaches. As I've mentioned, someone at the television station in Burnaby that we won't talk about counted the number of stories I had done in Stanley Park. She stopped at one thousand.

Many were about gardeners. One was on a woman who worked with a rake by day but did something else at night. She was a pole dancer, and for us she demonstrated on a steel pole with a traffic sign at the top.

With her work boots on and her rough clothing, she climbed the pole and raised her legs and then slid beautifully down before moving up without showing any effort. You try that. I could barely hold on.

The story was beautiful (humbly I say that) and much commented upon.

And speaking of boots, which I just did, (you have to go back a few lines, to before the sliding up and down the pole, which if you are a guy is the only thing you were thinking about and if you are a woman you were thinking "I could do that if I had a pole with a traffic sign in my basement") . . .

Anyway, speaking of boots, the gardeners have the most wonderful way of retiring. Just outside their lunchroom in the park they have a pole and on it are hung the boots of all the retired gardeners. Some have been there for years. They are tied on by their laces.

The pole is high, higher than the one-storey roof of the lunchroom. It has many boots on it. All are filled with rainwater. Most have moss growing on them. If you look closely enough you can see the soles separating from the boots. That would be a sign of passing into a new place in time and space.

I put this story on television when Rick the gardener retired. He was a wonderful guy. One of the best stories with him was about the fellow who was sad when he brought his wife's ashes into the park to spread them around the flowers that she loved so much.

Before he could do that, this fellow, according to Rick, met the old keeper of the Nine o'Clock Gun. The old gun keeper loved his gun and his rum. He was sitting on a bench near the cannon when the fellow with the ashes came into the park. The fellow with the ashes looked sad.

"Want a drink?" asked the keeper of the gun.

"Just a sip," said the man with the ashes.

The sip, as sips always do, turned into a swig and then a gulp and then a heads-back swallow.

The short of this story is the man with the ashes, with the help of the man with the cannon, put his wife's remains into the cannon and at nine p.m. precisely they both sent her into the beauty of the afterlife with more of a kick than she may have ever known in life. Or maybe not. We don't know.

Anyway, we did a story about Rick hanging up his boots when he retired. As a side note, this lifelong gardener of a thousand acres lives in a small apartment in North Vancouver and has a few plants on his balcony. He is one of the most gentle souls I have ever met.

I have another story about Rick. He is in one of the previous books so please, if you have read this, forgive me. If you haven't, it's a beautiful story.

I watched one woman pushing another in a wheelchair come into the park. They did this every day. The woman pushing was young. The woman in the chair was old, very old.

Rick and I were talking near the Rose Garden when he saw them.

"Oh, my heavens, I forgot," he said.

He broke away from our conversation and ran, yes he literally ran back to a building. I watched him furiously clipping and then he ran back to me.

"I always give her a flower," he said, and then he trotted down a path in the garden to meet the women.

I saw him hand the one in the wheelchair the flower. They talked for just a few seconds and then the two women continued on their walk.

Rick came back to me.

"They come every Wednesday."

"And you give her a flower?"

He just nodded and smiled.

"Do you know them?" I asked.

"No. I saw them a few months ago and gave her a flower and I've been doing it ever since."

The following Wednesday I was waiting with a cameraman. It took a while to talk Rick into it. He didn't want to look like he was bragging about what he was doing, but I told him people would think the whole thing was wonderful and they would feel good. He agreed so long as the woman in the wheelchair got most of the attention.

No problem.

As it turned out she just wanted to thank him, and everyone felt good.

Rick is retired now and his boots are hung on the pole and I still say thank you whenever I think of him.

But then things changed. The Park Board developed new policies for itself. No gardener, no employee, could talk to any reporter without the official permission of the media relations department.

I learned of this when I was asking a lifeguard about the weather.

"Can't talk to you," he said.

"You're kidding," I said.

"No," he said.

I called the media relations department. I was told I could talk to the lifeguard if I submitted my questions to the official in the department and if there was a spokesperson from the department at the scene.

"You're kidding," I said.

"No. That's the policy," she said.

"Suppose I only want to ask about planting tulips?" I said.

"You need permission," she said.

"Why?" I asked.

"Policy," she said.

"That's crazy," I said.

"I won't talk to you if you get personal," she said.

That ended the conversation, but I found out later that all the gardeners had been told in writing that they couldn't talk to anyone in the media.

I mentioned to the media people that I had been doing okay without them for thirty-five years and had said nice things about the parks.

They said no exceptions to the policy

Later a new person in charge relented and said I could talk to the gardeners *if* I called the media relations department ahead of time. Then they would call the gardeners and tell them it was okay for me to talk to them and then they would answer my questions if they felt the questions were appropriate.

The gardeners also know that there's a sheet of paper on the wall in their work stations and it says they cannot talk to a reporter.

I hate to bring my problems to you—yes, you reading—and this is the only time I'll do this, but it is important you know the extent to which government organizations control their employees. I understand private companies doing this because they are private, but the Park Board is paid by the public, you and me. Their job is to serve the public, mostly by making the parks pretty, but now, as a gatherer of information for the public, I cannot gather information, not even about tulips and dandelions and the weather.

I also cannot spontaneously ask a gardener a question about worms or the colour of leaves to see if there is something fascinating about it to tell you. First I would have to get permission to ask, then they would have to be told they can answer, then they would have to decide if they might get into trouble by answering, and then they might say, "No, nothing new with worms or the colour of leaves."

You may or may not have noticed that over the last four years there have been no gardeners in any story. They still do nice things, I know, and I like them so much, but there have been no tales of how one would pick flowers for a woman in a wheelchair or how another woman's ashes were fired from a cannon or how one can dance on a pole while still wearing her coveralls and work boots.

It is a shame what bureaucrats can do.

However, there is one person who defies the rule. He is Tom, the lifeguard at Third Beach.

"I'm too old to worry," he said.

Now what kind of secrets did he reveal?

"You should have been here *two* minutes ago!" he said.

The way he said it we knew we really should have.

"The deer, you know the deer, was right here, right where you're standing. It was close enough for me to touch."

He raised his hands. "It was this close," he said holding his hands this far apart, which you know even without seeing it was not very far.

"He was beautiful, although he's probably a she, but I'm only guessing," said Tom, who can save lives better than he can analyze the sex of a beautiful wild creature that was this close to him.

All of this talking, of course, is breaking rules and regulations, and all of it Jim is videotaping, bless him.

"She came right out of the woods, right over there," said Tom walking there and pointing there. "Then she came up to here," he said returning to here.

"Oh, I wish you could have seen it. You could have gotten such good pictures."

Oh, let us second that. But something almost as good, or maybe better, was happening that we *were* getting sound and pictures of. We were watching the thrill and excitement of a person who just *two* minutes ago experienced something that most of us never do.

By the way, I know that if you live in the country and see deer every day you are saying this no big deal, and you are right—for you, but not for those of us who live in artificial worlds where wildlife is attached by a leash and we take it out to poop once a day on artificial grass.

A deer, close up, is amazing and exciting and wonderful and thrilling and even more than that. And we could share it.

"You know you're not supposed to talk to us without prior permission," I said.

He gave me one of those looks, the kind where you furrow your eyebrows and tilt your head and squeeze your lips together that says in the universal language, "Are you kidding?"

According to the regulations I should have called the Park Board and asked them if I could talk to Tom about the deer. I would ask him only about the deer. No questions, I promise, about the national economy or the budget for the park. The official I spoke to would say she would get back to me.

Now, full disclosure, as they say. I have been told after many conversations with the media department that I have been given dispensation by the board commissioner to do any stories I want once

I call. They will not have a representative nearby to check the questions and answers but I still have to call. Then a call will be made to the person I want to talk to. Spontaneous and happy answers, no. Bureaucrat-approved answers, yes.

However, what would have happened if another reporter had asked another lifeguard about the deer? First, the phone call. That may be followed by a meeting, because meetings are important. Then a call would be made to the lifeguard from headquarters telling him that he could talk to the reporter as soon as a representative from the office arrived.

Then the reporter would get a call saying he/she could schedule an interview for an hour later.

Then the reporter would ask the lifeguard, "What did you see?"

Lifeguard: "I saw a deer."

Reporter: "How close were you?"

Lifeguard looks at media representative to see if closeness would violate rules on being too close to wildlife. Media representative nods. This is an exceptional case where rules can be bent.

Lifeguard: "I would estimate a metre."

Reporter: "That is close."

Media representative shakes head. "That is a subjective question. 'How close is too close?' Please withdraw it."

Reporter to representative: "May I ask if it was exciting? That also requires a personal evaluation."

Media representative: "Of course. A Park Board employee is allowed to express emotions."

Reporter: "Exciting?"

Lifeguard: "Yes."

And the official would say, "I hope you are getting what you want."

Again, if this was me this is where I would explode. You would find bits of me all over the lifeguard station and all over the parking lot and especially all over the official and she would say, "See, the media just can't help sensationalizing."

But Tom saved us.

With one picture of the back of the deer at the beginning of the story and then Tom's full-frontal free and happy excitement and then another picture of the deer going away at the end it was a beautiful story.

And the officials never said a word.

Sadly, the deer was hit by a car a few days later. I wish I didn't have to tell you that. A press release from the Park Board announced its demise.

There is an addendum to this story. When you get mad at someone something else always seems to happen that makes you say that someone is not so bad and maybe you were wrong. And then you think about it and say, No, you were right.

After avoiding stories on Park Board employees and indoor recreation centres for years, something happened. I got a request to do a story about a choir of white-haired folk (so of course I like them).

They would be having a rehearsal. Good, I say. In the Roundhouse. Bad, I say.

The Roundhouse is the comfortable retirement home for Engine 374, the steam engine that united Canada long ago. Its picture is on the cover of *Haunting Vancouver*, my history of the city.

It is also where I met Cathy and Ed, she in a wheelchair, he in a snow-white beard but, more importantly, they in love. Their story is in my free book mentioned earlier and in *Unlikely Love Stories*.

When we go in the railroad side of the Roundhouse no one says "No," but the other end of the building is the community centre and it's closely guarded by the Park Board. The new rules there say, shout, bellow, "*No*, you, a reporter, can't enter without permission."

I used to wander in there at least once a week to see what was odd or sweet or beautiful. The people who ran it were nice. They would give me hints about lovable oddballs.

There was the barefoot ping-pong player who believed the ping of the ball was mystical, and there was the ten-year-old girl who had been going to the centre "all my life."

With her mother's permission she took us on a tour of her art room and ballet room and we went into "that room over there, but I don't know what they do in there." When we walked out she said, "I still don't know what they do in there."

And there was the indoor traffic jam in the stroller park near the centre's preschool.

It was all fun, and none of the stories could have been found by getting permission beforehand and being asked what story we will be doing.

"What story will you be doing?"

"We don't know."

"Well, then how can we give you permission to do a story about something that you don't know?"

Now let's jump back to the singing group. I don't want to let them down so I take a deep breath and call the Park Board to be allowed to enter the otherwise off limits of the community centre half of the Roundhouse.

The Park Board has won and they know it.

"Yes, of course you can enter. What time will you be there? Who are you going to see? Have they given you permission to tape them? Is there anything we can provide you with to make it easier? Glad you called."

The Roundhouse staff were waiting. They opened the door for us. There was a welcoming committee.

"Can we guide you to the rehearsal room? Do you need anything?"

The story was fine.

Later there was an email from the Park Board asking whether everything had been satisfactory.

All I had to do was call, so what am I complaining about?

Freedom. The freedom to talk to whomever I want without permission and to discover things I don't know exist and then to tell you about them. That is a big thing. That is my complaint.

The Race

Darn, I am late again and it is not my fault.

That's what I've been saying most of my life. It is the fault of the toaster that didn't toast or the sock that wasn't on my foot when I went to put on my shoe. I thought I had it and now I don't know where it is and I can't go to work with one sock. Someone would notice and say: "Hey, you only have one sock."

And I would say: "Oh, yeah? I didn't notice."

And he would say, "How can you not notice you only have one sock?"

From there on it would just get worse so I had to find my other sock, which was probably wrapped in the underpants that I took out of the dryer just a few minutes ago.

Yes, I know, I could get another pair of socks, but then do I take just one of that pair? For sure it won't match the one I have on. One will be longer than the other and if I sit someone might say, "Hey, your socks don't match."

Or they might be polite and not say it, but I would have to be careful about sitting because while I'm not big on fashion I don't want to look like an old man who can't get his socks to match.

But today there was another reason I was late. The Lions Gate Bridge. Okay, you are with me now. You know you can't get over it in the morning and you can't get over it in the afternoon. And it's hard the rest of the day.

More than forty years ago when I was new in Vancouver I covered a story for the *Sun* about plans to widen the bridge. I could not believe, and I truly mean that, I could not believe there was a three-lane bridge as basically the only way to get into the heart of the city.

I remember some people at the meeting saying this craziness has gone on for too long. Something *must* be done.

More than forty years later I was on the bridge, not moving. Politicians, residents, drivers, anyone with a life is still saying, "Something *must* be done!"

I usually take the Second Narrows, which is now called the Ironworkers. It is also crowded but at least you have a slim chance of getting across in reasonable time, sometimes.

But your odds on the Lions Gate are like betting on a 100:1 outsider at the track. Brave but not bright.

I was on the bridge because my wife had to get something at Park Royal before going to work. "Okay, we'll leave early, you whip into the store, I'll wait in the parking lot and in a few minutes we'll be on our way."

Okay, here's my two dollars on the 100:1 outsider.

I get a text from Jim Fong who did so well with the rear end of the deer: "Waiting in front of post office."

Neat. I can read the text because we are not moving but soon we will because . . . because I have faith in the impossible. Maybe they will open the second lane going south so some of us will stop yelling at our windshields.

We get up to the bridge deck. I ask my wife to text back. "Just say 'Soon. Thanks.'"

We crawl. I don't have to explain it. You've been there.

We get to Georgia Street. It has been fifteen minutes since we left Park Royal.

I get another text: "Soon?"

I ask my wife to write back. "Just make three dots and say '. . . as possible.'"

We don't move at all. No one moves. You've been there too.

Ten minutes and we are just crossing Denman Street. "We could walk faster," I say.

Ten minutes later (no exaggeration; I know because I have someone who is going to be late for work sitting next to me) we are passing White Spot. We could have walked here faster on our hands; even though that would have been impossible it still would have been faster.

Ten more minutes and another text: "Should I wait?"

This is not good. He has been there half an hour. Once he's finished working with me he has other stories to shoot and before he can do that we have to find something to put into the camera.

Ten more minutes! This is impossible! My wife gets out and walks to work. That will be faster. Then suddenly, of course, an IDEA. You've been waiting for this sudden bit of optimism, I know. Somehow the sun will come out, right, because it almost always does in these stories. Well, here it is, the big idea. Walking! That's today's story.

In five minutes I am at the post office. It is just a meeting place, and now we are three-quarters of an hour late in starting, but what an opportunity!

I have seen that there is construction (surprise!) on Georgia just past Granville. Good. Nothing will change.

Jim and I go to Thurlow Street, one block west of Burrard. "There! There's a guy pushing a baby stroller," I say. "He's our winner, I hope."

Jim follows him, from behind, going from the stroller to the cars and back to the stroller.

"The stroller is in the lead. The stroller is nose and nose with the BMW. The stroller is pulling ahead."

During the race we are able to talk to several people in cars. This is possible because the cars are either not moving or not moving fast enough to be called moving.

"Tell your boss why you are late," I say.

They tell him on the camera.

"Tell your politicians what you think."

They tell them.

"The stroller is closing in on the Bentley with the N on the back."

Have you seen how many Bentleys there are with Ns? No wonder most of us can't afford to live in Vancouver.

But it is wonderful, exciting, amazing to see the trotter, that would be the stroller, moving ahead of the thoroughbreds. This is the 100:1 shot not just showing up the high-priced talent but wiping the floor with them.

Plus we are giving visual backup proof to the excuse many would have for being late. This is community service TV.

And now they are heading to the finish line—that would be the crosswalk at Burrard Street.

"The stroller is in the lead. The stroller is moving ahead. The stroller *wins!!*"

The script was written for me by the race.

Jim and I were done. He could go on to the police press conference about the murder the night before. And, outside of that, I was happy. You can't be happy about murders but on the Georgia Street racetrack the long shot was the winner. That is happiness.

One last thing. The hero, the jockey behind the baby on wheels, was anonymous, as many heroes are. We never saw his face. He waited for the light and crossed Burrard Street way ahead of the cars he was up against, including the Bentley, and went on to the winner's circle, wherever that was—probably meeting his wife who wanted to know why he was late.

The Racetrack

Speaking of the track, which we are now, it is my favourite place, but a few things first:

I don't like gambling. My wife and I do gamble but it is always on who do you think is on the other end of the blinking light on the answering machine on the phone, or will we have anything besides bills in the mail when we get home? We always bet a quarter and we never pay, but I like the idea that you have to make a choice on something that you have no control over. It's a game.

The track is different. It is a passion, both for me and for the thousands who think they can out-think a horse, which is impossible.

To stand by the last turn before they head into the stretch for the finish line is everything every sport wished they had. You can feel the earth move. That is pretty good when you are standing up with your clothes on.

You can watch half a dozen animals and humans trying to win, and I have been around the track long enough to know that the horses want to win. It is the alpha something or other but they want to be first so that the other horses know they are standing next to the top dog. They are so human.

You can bet or not. The track is free to get in once you've paid that overpriced fee for parking. It has also become trendy for young whatever their generation is called. They dress in good clothing—suits, pretty dresses and hats, lots of hats for the women, so many hats that there are hat sellers there for those who don't have hats, which is the only sure way of making money at the track. They aren't really hats so much as tiny tufts of feathers that don't cover any part of a head, made famous by the famous races in England where they wear them.

There are also food carts and beer and wine and music, but most of all there are six or seven strong animals and an equal number of men and women who will risk their lives trying to be first.

That sounds like the Roman coliseum with fights to the death. There hasn't been a death at the track in twenty years but it is still scary.

The horses run at nearly 60 kilometres an hour, which means they are flying while the riders are holding on with only their ankles. You try that. The other horses are almost touching them but not quite, because that is illegal. Their hoofs are below. If a jockey falls the next step is a trampling.

If it is muddy the riders have goggles. As the mud gets thrown up their goggles get covered and they are blinded, so they lift one hand and throw off their goggles and under it is another pair—and another pair. Five, six times during a race their faces are smeared with mud and they grab for a way to see.

There is a difference in the summer when it's hot and dry. There is no problem about dust, but there is the weight. The jockeys are weighed before each race. Weight is a big thing in horse racing. The horses have to carry it.

If a jockey loses, and remember all of them do except one, the owners and the trainers want to know why.

First of all they check the weight. Did the jockey gain anything between the first race and the second? By anything they mean a few grams. In imperial measurement it's less.

So to keep their weight down the jockeys, even on the hottest days, each buy a can of 7 Up or ginger ale. They poke a tiny hole in the top and when they are desperate for a drink of water they suck the fizz off the can. No weight gain. Sports are tough.

All they have to do to explain why they lost is to blame the horse or the horses that were in front of them, but there was one they never blamed—George Royal. If you go to the track, and you should because at least the first time you will think this is the greatest thing there is, you will see a frozen-in-time statue of a horse in the paddock.

The paddock is where the horses parade around in a circle while the betters watch them and think they can tell a winner by the muscles or tails or ears.

Actually, the most prized way of picking a winner is to wait for the horse that poops the last. He or she feels the best, as you know, and will run the fastest. Sometimes it works.

Anyway, in the middle of the paddock is this statue. It looks like any in a herd of four-legged animals with a head and tail, but it is George Royal. He ran at the Pacific National Exhibition racetrack in the 1960s. Think of Babe Ruth. Think of Wayne Gretzky. There are many other names but you get the idea.

George Royal, a Canadian horse, a British Columbian horse, in the world of horses was a nothing. "He's from where? Can't run."

George Royal would stand at the gate waiting for the start and then, bang! And he would still be standing there. Go horse! Nothing. All the horses would be pounding their hearts out on the track—except George Royal.

Then George Royal, no matter who was the jockey on his back, would take a few steps. The crowd would groan. He's a loser, even though they had bet on him.

Then he would take a few more steps, and a few more, and he would gallop and he would push his hoofs into the dirt and charge and he would gain speed and push harder and in a few moments he would be at the back of the pack of his competition.

But that was halfway around the track and horses at the back at the halfway mark are losers.

Then George Royal would dig his hoofs in deeper and use muscles that no one could see. He pushed and he flew. He moved onto the outside. No horse or car racer or ice skating racer goes on the outside, but George Royal went on the outside.

And he passed the horses at the back. He flew faster and passed the horses at the middle of the pack. Then he took off and passed the horses at the front while he was still on the outside, which meant he was running farther than they were.

And then at the last turn, where I said you should stand to see the true moment of pain and triumph, George Royal would pull in front of the pack and that is where he let it all hang out, as they say now.

He didn't win by a nose or a head; he was alone as he went for the finish line. He probably didn't know where that was but he knew that somewhere up ahead he would be reined back while the other horses were still trying to get there.

Good feeling.

He did this over and over, so many times that he was upgraded and moved to California where he did the same thing again. California of course has much better tracks with the much better horses. That didn't matter. They were running. George Royal was flying.

When you see the statue of that plain old brown horse in the middle of the paddock remember that greatness can be anywhere. Then try to pick a winner.

One of my favourite people at the track was a groom who sang to the horses. He loved them and they loved him. Horses do love. And there was Ed Thompson. Okay, okay. You know the story, but every time I go to the track I tell it again.

I'll keep it short, but if you want proof that you get what you want, look at Ed.

He was a banker, and an executive-type banker, in a ridiculous place to be an executive in a suit: Dawson City in the Yukon. A cold place, but he was hot in his rise up the ranks of important people in the bank. From the Yukon he would be transferred to a high-class place like Vancouver, but Ed didn't want that. He, for reasons known only to him, wanted to be around horses, and the horses he wanted to be with were racehorses.

He loved them. If you don't want your daughter to grow up to be a groom and then a trainer and then an internationally famous and rich jockey don't take her to the track.

Ed wanted to be with horses. He quit his job at the bank. His friends said, "Ed, you are a nutcase." They said other things but this is a family book.

He moved to Vancouver and walked into the barns at the back of the track.

"Want something?" someone asked.

"I want to work here," he said.

He got a job. It isn't hard to get a job there. If you want work go to the track. You can start out walking the horses. After they run they have to cool off, slowly. You take the bridle and walk around and around inside the barns. And then you walk some more. It takes a long time for a horse to slowly cool down. And when you are finished you walk another horse. Don't ask about how much you will get paid. You can afford to eat and you don't need a gym membership.

And then you get promoted. You are a groom. You get to brush and feed and wash and water and carry hay and then you get to clean out the stalls.

You get to sleep in the barns, usually in a tiny room with no windows next to the horses. You are there in case a horse wakes up in the middle of the night and you have to care for it. And somewhere down the row of stables one horse will wake up every night.

That is where Ed was sleeping and working, and when he did

finally get to sleep he was up again at 4:45 a.m. because the day begins at 5.

This is what Ed wanted. In truth, everyone who works at the track wants this because if they didn't want it they would actually be crazy, not just called crazy by those who would never do this work.

In time he got a chance to train a horse. Trainers are the artists of the track. They bring out what is in those incredible animals that have such heart. It is all done through long, cold, wet mornings on the track with exercise riders who ride as the trainers tell them. Faster here, hold back there; like training any athlete except these can't talk.

By the time I met Ed he was one of the top ten trainers at Hastings Park. He never missed the bank. What Ed did—following his dreams right through the muck and manure—is what I wish for everyone, minus the muck and manure.

His story is not very different from Reilly's, except I saw him catch his winner.

There is more to the story. It involves love, which changes everything. You can read it in the book I gave away and you can get through the internet. The email address is in the Foreword.

Ed is retired now. He plays Santa Claus at Christmas. Santa never wanted to be in banking.

Flowers for Joe

People also die. Almost always there is emotion, but sometimes it sneaks up on you. We did not know about the death or the feeling or anything.

Murray Titus and I were on Denman Street looking for something bright on a gloomy November day. He had a camera on his shoulder and I had hope in my head, and just as you have to remove the lens cap on the camera to get anything you have to open your eyes to everything and anything.

"Would you take pictures of that corner store, please?"

Always say please and thank you. If you learned that as a child you got much further in life than you can imagine.

The store was across the street and it was surrounded by flowers. This is something we all know, we just have to notice. Most corner stores in this part of the world have gardens on their sidewalks. That is a local kind of magic.

They are wrapped flowers and potted flowers and then more of both. There are bright and subtle colours and green, lots of green, even on a gloomy November day.

This will be good, I think. You don't need a garden if you have a corner store nearby. Murray takes close-ups and medium shots and at least one wide shot.

It is a fundamental rule for photography or life. Of course it is or we wouldn't put it in here. If you want to get to know things, look at the overall scene, then move in a little closer and then get right in there next to it so that you are almost brushing the petals or looking at the perfect imperfections.

Alongside the close-ups of the flowers are always the price tags. Okay, ignore them, you are just looking and enjoying.

And then there was a man looking at the flowers. He didn't look like the flower type. He was more round than thin and more short than tall, like most of us. He had on a baseball cap and a kind of sports bomber jacket. I don't remember what team.

Anyone can buy flowers but in a world full of prejudging he didn't look like he was buying them for himself. On the other side of unfair evaluation, if he was buying them for a wife it would be a beautiful moment.

I could see him telling us how much his wife would be surprised. It was her birthday, their anniversary. He did this once a year and always came to this store and she liked yellow or pink or whatever colour he was looking for.

I like my dreams. Even if they fall apart I have them for a moment.

"Hello. Hate to bother you." The usual stuff.

No. Not for his wife. He was not married. And no, not for himself. For a friend.

That is even better, I think. No, I know it is better if he will not be too embarrassed and tell us.

"My friend Joe."

He said it while still looking down at the flowers and picking up one potted plant then putting it down.

"Who is Joe?" can we ask.

"My friend," he said.

"Would we be imposing if we asked you about Joe?"

Some things are very hard to ask and you have to ask permission, and when you ask you have to be truly humble. Spotting a phony or a salesman is easy. They don't know humble from a hole in the ground.

"Sure," he said. "We met in a bar a long time ago. He was a little older than me, and big. A very big man."

One word in the past tense and the story changes.

"Is he not here any more?"

"No, he died a long time ago."

He went back to looking at the flowers, picking up one, putting it down, then picking up another. The flowers were more important than us.

He told us his name, Ralph, and he had worked in a warehouse. I didn't understand if it was part of a grocery store or something else. Joe had worked in the office of some shipping company. I didn't get the name of the business.

"We would talk all the time. We went to a bar usually but sometimes we would go to his apartment and talk. And in the summer we would meet on that bench across the street," he pointed at the bench, "and drink coffee."

Ralph was back in another world. Daydreams are a good place to go when the day is gloomy.

"We even went on a bus trip together down to Seattle. He wasn't married either. He had never been married."

I asked if the flowers were for his grave.

"Yes," he said, and then suddenly, out of nowhere, he grabbed a fairly large pot of yellow chrysanthemums, like he didn't want anyone else to get it.

"You like that?"

"This is what I want."

It wasn't light or easy to carry. If he held it in both hands by his stomach the flowers came up to his chin.

He went into the store and paid. We waited until he came out.

"Is the cemetery near here?" I asked.

"It's in Surrey."

"Driving?"

No, taking a bus, several buses and the SkyTrain in between, he said.

"When did he die?"

"Eight years ago."

"You go once a year?"

"No, every month."

"For eight years?"

"Every month."

Nothing else to ask. We watched him walk north on Denman to get a bus on Georgia Street to visit his friend named Joe.

In the darkroom where the editing is done a young fellow named Ryan was putting together the pictures. He was touched, of course, by the story, but in his world his wife was about to have a baby, their first. He was bubbling with the excitement we all have at the beginning. And now he was looking at the pictures of the end of the journey.

"Life is really precious, isn't it?" he said.

He knew that of course, but there are things that sometimes happen that do more than remind us of it, they let us feel it. And then it always seems there is nothing else you have to know.

Kite Lady

We were wandering. It is good to wander. We were exploring. It is also good to do that. Exploring sometimes lets you find something new and when you do you get excited.

Everyone does that. You can walk down a street two blocks from where you live and see a house, a garden, a pile of garbage or someone picking up garbage and say, "This is neat. How come I've never seen this before?"

That's because you have been a stick-in-the-mud. No, that is wrong. I can't call you that after you bought his book, but face it, if you haven't walked on a street two blocks from where you live and you have lived there for more than a week, you are a . . . stick-in-the-mud.

I was with Murray Titus, again. You have read about him before. He is no stick-in-the-anything, but wait.

"You have never been to Burkeville?"

"Nope."

How is that possible? You are a news cameraman. You go everywhere. You went to the war in Bosnia with a helmet and a bulletproof vest along with your camera. You sometimes see death and destruction for breakfast. You are an actual street-wise journalist. You seldom go inside. You are at those events that alter and illuminate our times.

Walter Cronkite from CBS used to say that. "Today was a day like all days, filled with those events that alter and illuminate our times."

That was, to me, the line that elevated journalism to poetry and philosophy. And there it was on television in black and white said by someone who brought the news of the day to everyone, at least everyone in America and the part of Canada that was close enough to the border to get the signal.

Some reading this now are saying, "Who's Walter Cronkite?" and "I never heard anyone say that and, in addition, what the heck is black and white?"

For you who never enjoyed the beauty of black and white, black and white was *I Love Lucy*, and the Vietnam War. It was everything.

Paul Simon said that everything looks better in black and white, but he was also singing about Kodachrome, which was film, colour film, which some of you know nothing about.

Film was something you put in your camera and when you finished a roll you took it out and brought it to a photo lab or London Drugs and waited a few days and you got your pictures and you opened the envelope before you walked out of the store and you said, "Wow. This is wonderful. This is Uncle Ned and oh, no. I shook the camera when I took a picture of the new baby."

If you look at your grandparents' old photo albums you will see some black and white pictures. They are small. They are of people you've heard about. Most of those people are no longer here but their pictures are in your hands, which is neat.

Those were the days when pictures were precious. You took twelve of them. When the rolls got longer there were twenty-four, and then thirty-six.

It took you weeks to get through that roll.

Now you click a hundred times at a child's birthday party. You skim through them faster than a blur and stop at one or two and they stay in your camera or phone for, well, forever until you have too many and download them onto your computer where they meet with thousands of other pictures that are there, just there, and largely forgotten.

With film you held the photos, showed them, put them in an album and then opened the album on special occasions. And everyone said, "I remember Uncle Ned. He was so nice."

They were different times. That is when, in black and white, Walter Cronkite said, "President Kennedy is dead," and the world went into shock.

Black and white, twelve pictures to the roll, was when Burkeville was born. It was during the Second World War and airplanes were a big and sadly disposable weapon.

Many were built by Boeing in the old hangars at Vancouver's airport, which was then just a small landing strip, and to keep the workers from taking hours to get to the plant, the federal government built a town at the end of the runway and named it after the president of Boeing, Stanley Burke. If you ever get that question on a test you can wow them.

At that time the little airport was out in the sticks. The only things in Richmond, just across one of the fingers of the Fraser River, were farms, and going the other way, across the Fraser in South Vancouver were mud flats.

The federal Wartime Housing department cut streets into the bush at the end of the landing strip and built tiny houses and rented them cheaply to the workers, who could now walk to the hangars. After the war the houses were sold to veterans.

Nowhere on earth is there a town that looks more idyllic. Norman Rockwell (don't ask, just look on Google) would pray for a town like this. This was middle Canada, middle America, the pretend middle of anywhere that only exists in paintings, never in photos, because no place like this really exists.

There were ditches with a wooden bridge in front of each garden.

The houses were cozy—that's another way of saying they were either four or six rooms. The backyards had chickens and the front yards had children.

The curved streets were named after airplanes: Wellington, Anson, Catalina.

Seventy years later it is still the same.

Two other things about it stand out. Firstly it is the only place people live on Sea Island. There is only Burkeville and the airport. It has no mall, no stores, no gas station, no laundromat, no library, no medical marijuana dispensary, no traffic lights and no sushi restaurants. In short, it's a really nice place.

Secondly it has just one minor drawback. The little airstrip right next to it is now a giant runway with 747s landing on it and they go over the houses so low they only just miss the roofs. At full throttle the engines blanket the town with thunder, and it can happen every couple of minutes.

Okay, you can't have everything.

"I don't hear a thing," said Lou, who is big and friendly and lives on a corner lot and has plaster people with pointed hats all around his yard.

Lou has character. Lou and his wife, Linda, always have clothes on the line, even in the rain, even in the winter when it rains for weeks.

"It was good enough for my mother in Manitoba so it's good enough for me," says Linda.

They are deliciously cool characters, like many who live in Burkeville, and I was looking for them to introduce to Murray so Murray would believe me that there are characters here and so we could put Lou and Linda on television and earn our pay.

Knock, knock.

Please be home. Knock. He's not home.

"They're not home," said a neighbour walking down the country street. "They never go out, but today they're out."

But I can't hear this neighbour. An airplane is landing overhead and I don't mean it is landing just beyond the town. I mean it is landing overhead. It is just that it misses the little town by an arm's length and touches down on the runway just on the other side of the fence that ends the town. Close, I thought.

"What'd you say?" I shout.

"He's not home," said the neighbour. "And you don't have to shout. Just wait, then talk."

Neighbours know when to talk and when someone is out.

"How do you stand the noise?" I ask.

"We don't hear it," said the neighbour.

That's what Lou said when I first met him. "What noise?"

We go on. I know there is a woman who lives at the end of a dead-end road where no one passes by. She puts her dahlias out front in jars and sells them. The sign says: "Flowers $2 a bunch. Please leave the jar."

Knock, knock. She's not home.

What is going on? The only people I know in Burkeville are not home.

We drive around but we don't go far because you could walk across town in five minutes. Then we see a woman with white hair that has a red patch at the back.

"Beautiful," I say to Murray as a plane is landing.

He doesn't take his eyes off the road or the plane, both of which he can see without moving his eyes. He didn't hear me.

"Beautiful," I say again.

He looks at me. "Let's talk to her," he says. "She looks interesting."

"Good idea," I whisper.

She turns out to be the kite lady. The red dye forms a maple leaf in the shape of a kite. She makes kites, she flies kites, she has a trunk load of kites in her car.

She brings a tiny one out from her tiny pretty house. The string goes over her finger and the kite flies up by her shoulder.

She teaches kite-making in schools. She is wonderful.

"Could we see you fly a big one?" I ask.

She shakes her head. "No, it's against the law."

"Say what?"

"Can't fly anything this close to the airport," she says as a flying aluminum tube with three hundred people inside slides overhead just out of reach. The ground vibrates. She smiles. I am thrilled.

The kite lady who can't fly her kites. Stop the presses. The story is good.

"I want to show this place to my girlfriend," said Murray.

If you get a chance go visit Burkeville. It's on the way to the South Terminal, which was once the only terminal. A sign will say: Burkeville.

Take a look, visit Lou, buy some dahlias, but don't fly a kite.

The Swimmer

What I like most about the man with the booties and gloves is that he doesn't do what he does for publicity. He is totally quiet about being a nutcase—a brave, determined, unflinching, admirable nutcase.

Pete Cline and I met him after Pete apologized for wasting our time. He is the camera guy who took incredible pictures of the hands of two veterans in the story about John the Barber and the Gerry the Gardener. He knows his way around a camera.

On the morning of January 21 last year he suggested we go around the park. Halfway around Stanley Park on any morning in late January of any year you see the same thing. Nothing.

Sane folks, even joggers who are not, are smart enough to avoid icy paths, cold rain and dark skies with a promise of more icy paths.

"Sorry," he said.

"No problem," I said, trying to believe what I was saying.

We went to Third Beach where Tom the lifeguard works, but he

230

only works there when people go swimming. No swimmers, no lives to save.

Pete parked and I walked ahead of him. I always do this at Third Beach because their bathroom is open year round. No matter what I think of the Park Board I thank them endlessly for their open-door policy.

It is raining. I am under my umbrella looking down at the beach, which even on a good day in the winter is almost always empty—and this is not a good day.

"Whoa," said I out loud in a way even more thankful than for an unlocked bathroom.

"I'll get my camera," said Pete.

There was a man in a bathing suit coming out of the water.

Pete is large. He ran. I also am too large for my frame, but I jumped. You know the way a five-year-old jumps when something exciting happens? You don't? Well then go look at a five-year-old when something exciting happens. You see what he/she does? Now look at me. Yes. Embarrassing.

We go down the long steps to the sand and then in city shoes walk across the wet, sticky beach. The wet, sticky beach goes over the tops of my shoes and slips down onto my socks.

"Hello, we don't want to bother you," I say.

That is fairly ridiculous. There is no one else in sight, we are talking to the only person besides us down here and we are obviously bothering him. To say we don't want to do this is a stretch.

He is kind.

"It's okay," he says.

My questions are asked without periods or commas. "Why when who and again why?"

He is not slender. He is not a competitive swimmer. He is not young. In short, he is wonderful.

"I do it every day," he says.

His name is Mike. "It's refreshing."

"No matter what mood you are in before you go in, you are in a better mood when you come out."

This is better than Dr. Phil, I think. He just leaves you crying.

Mike was wearing gloves and booties. "Too cold to walk on the sand and too cold on the fingers."

Then he laughed and said, "I wear a swim cap when it snows, otherwise I'd look like an ice cream cone."

But what I liked most about him was he was doing this where no one was likely to see him. He wasn't doing it for publicity and nor was he doing it to get into conversations about why he was doing it. For this we apologized. He was now getting both.

He was doing it for himself. Anything you do for that reason has extra rewards.

"If I am stressed when I go in I am not stressed when I come out."

Better than rows of books on how to de-stress yourself. They just leave you trying to breathe deeply while emptying your mind while not thinking about those things that stress you. Don't think about them. Just don't. *Don't! Don't think!!*

And then he left, in the rain, walking over the wet, cold, sticky sand. He had only his towel over his shoulder. His car was in the parking lot, the only one there besides ours.

If it wasn't for Pete and me there would have been no one watching, and Mike had done this hundreds of times, hundreds and hundreds of times.

Anyone who does something just for the sake of doing it and not for the sake of being known for doing it is a master of the art, even if no one knows it.

There's one other little thing about Third Beach that you may already know from an earlier book but just in the remote possibility you did not get that book here's another chance to know it.

During World War II swimming was off limits. In fact the park was off limits for anyone except the army. Third Beach was the main point of defence against an attack by Japanese ships.

Cannons were lined up on the ridge high above the beach. Behind them, under the current parking lot of the Teahouse, was the store room for the artillery shells. If you look around right near the curb you will find a steel plate on the ground. That was the door that led to the brass shells and the steel projectiles and the gunpowder.

The Teahouse was the officers' dining room. If you go into the army make sure you are an officer. The grunts who did the work and loaded the cannons and peeled the potatoes lived in barracks in the beach parking lot.

If you stand now where the cannons were you will see many ships. Some are from Japan, carrying cars. Again, why do we bother with wars?

Walking

And one more thing about that same spot.

It had been a long time since Shawn Foss, a cameraman at CTV, had been to Third Beach. He had moved out to the Fraser Valley and had been working there. Now he was back and we were going through the park.

"This is where the cannons were," I told him as we drove by the Teahouse. "And down on Third Beach is where we will find a story for tonight."

We had only worked together a few times so I wanted to be really cocky. Plus if you can't find it at Third Beach you can always go on to Second Beach and just pretend you misspoke—and then run for public office.

Nothing on the beach, of course, because if you are going to be cocky you are going to get shot down. Remember what comes after pride. Oh, come on, yes you do. You at least know someone who went to church at least once.

Back to reality. Nothing. So if nothing works, turn around. This is another reference from that same source.

Long ago there was a fisherman who wasn't catching anything. He complained to his boss and the boss said, "Fish from the other side of the boat."

Pretty dumb solution, probably thought the fisherman, but you've got to do what the boss says, so he did. And his boat almost sank from the fish he caught.

There is a lesson here, believe it or not. If something isn't working, try something else. Turn around. Go ahead, try it.

We turned around and there was a fellow walking by—nothing distinctive about him but give him a try. After all, he is there, and never pass up a parking spot or an opportunity.

"Hello, hate to bother you . . ." The usual.

Yes, he is walking through the park. Yes he walks a lot, in fact every day. Yes, he walks 25 kilometres every day. Yes, he had just spent four hours walking with a friend who got tired and so now he was walking for another hour by himself.

And yes, he keeps track of it all with an app on his phone, which he would love to show us. This included how many steps he had climbed that morning. He had done the long stairway to Third Beach three times and now was going again.

And yes, Shawn would climb up and down with him getting pictures of his feet and all of him and then follow him from behind and then run ahead to get more pictures of him approaching.

"How did that happen?" Shawn asked after he left.

"Easy, we turned around," I said. "And now," because we had walked to the top parking lot near the Teahouse, I said, "if you turn around I'll show you where Pauline Johnson is buried."

"You don't know who Pauline Johnson is?"

And there began another story. She was once the most famous Canadian in the world; not just the most famous Canadian woman but the most famous Canadian. You can Google her or read my history book, *Haunting Vancouver*. That would make me happy.

Cars

Just a shorty—and it's about time. Most of these stories have been long and I apologize. This one is about cars, which I don't much care about.

I was at a friend's house today. His name is Chester Grant and he had a plaque on his wall of a 1957 Chevy, and it was blue.

"It's a classic," he said.

"I had one of those," I said. "A '57 Chevy, and it was blue."

"Wow, I'm envious," he said.

He said he had never had one and didn't know why he was given the plaque, but he hung it on his wall because everyone says, "Wow, that's a '57 Chevy."

He wanted to give it to me because, well, because I had had one and he had not.

"No, thank you," I said. "It looks so beautiful on your wall. Folks will be envious."

The real reason was that no one would be envious of my classic 1957 Chevrolet, which I didn't know was classic when I got it. It came from the factory with classic design, classic two-tone paint, classic powerful engine, classic easy shifting and, most of all, two upright fins above the rear fenders that looked like a pair of attacking sharks. Who wouldn't want to look like attacking sharks on the road?

My blue '57 Chevy was my first car but I didn't know how to drive when I got it. As you know I am from New York and kids in New York don't grow up with cars. There are millions of them on the streets and they made playing on those streets a challenge, but as for driving, we didn't do that.

Everyone took the subway and buses. Typical conversation between teenage boys riding on the subway:

"You ever getting a car?"

"Someday. But where would I park it?"

End of conversation.

Anyway, I was about to get married and I thought it would be good to drive my bride from the church to the hotel that we had booked for that night. That's what people did, I imagined. I could only imagine since I had never been married or driven a car.

To rent a car you had to be able to drive and you had to have a licence. That was two problems.

I found a driving school that advertised a three-hour refresher course. Good enough for me.

I paid, and in the first hour I learned how to go forward in a car with automatic transmission. The next day, the second hour, I learned how to turn. The third day and the third hour I learned how to back up and park. I also rented the car for a fourth hour to take a driving test which I had scheduled to follow the third hour.

"Really? I passed?" I said to the clerk who stamped a piece of paper and said this was my interim licence until my official one came in the mail.

Lesson: trust no one on the road.

An uncle of mine who drove buses for years and then taught others how to drive buses thought my plans lacked some basic intelligence. He drove us to the hotel.

Really boring so far, right? Sorry.

A month later I was in basic training in the Air Force with many others, mostly from the South where they had grown up with two birthrights—driving and shooting.

They couldn't believe I had never fired a rifle. They couldn't believe I couldn't hit a target. I wasn't going to tell them I had never shifted a gear.

That is when a sergeant said to me in an unkind way: "Boy, bring that truck over here."

The truck was big. I was small. I looked at it and thought no way can I push it. I climbed into the driver's seat. I was lost. This was not like the cars in the driving school.

So many pedals. And no letters with a D and N and P. I stared at them.

"Boy! Move that truck."

I looked out the window.

"I don't know how."

Two hundred pounds of sergeant with a red face walked toward me.

"You what?!"

"I don't know . . ."

I didn't finish before he said, "You useless subhuman waste of skin. You northerners know *nothing*."

I did not feel good.

"Slide your sorry ass over to the other side of that US Government issued truck and make room for a man who knows how to drive."

People sometimes aren't as kind as they should be.

I slid—at least I could do that—and a fellow trainee who was barely seventeen years old and looked younger hopped up into the cab. Yes, he hopped up like he had been doing that all his life, and he probably had.

This is two generations later and I still remember how he pushed down on one pedal and wiggled the mysterious stick in the middle and gunned the engine and then the truck moved.

I thought it was a miracle. I also thought you should never insult anyone.

But outside of trucks, I needed a car. I was living off the base with my wife. Suggestion to everyone in the military: don't get married just days before you put on a uniform.

Someone told me a '57 Chevy was for sale, cheap.

I liked half of that. Cheap was good. '57 Chevy was a mystery. I had no idea what that meant.

It was nose deep in a blackberry patch. I paid $150 for it. I sat inside.

Question. How do I move it back?

"Put it in reverse." I heard that from someone outside.

There was no R on the dashboard.

I now owned a car but I couldn't back up to drive it away. To these folks in the deep South that was like owning a rifle but not knowing how to load it. Impossible.

"How did you ever win the war?" the man selling me the car said. He meant the Civil War. That was when time stopped there.

I was worse than a failure. The friendly sergeant who drove me to the point of purchase said in a patient and understanding way: "You can't what?" He backed it out. He showed me the clutch and the gears.

Another lesson: patience is good, even when you can't believe the stupidity of the one you are being patient with. I still remember how kind he was.

Over the next few days I learned how to push down the clutch and shift and let the clutch up. I was a real driver.

However, there was another problem with this car. It had no floor. It had rotted out so when I drove I could watch the road under my feet. Now that would be called distracted driving. It was also bad in the rain.

I got hold of some sheet metal but I had no idea about riveting, welding, gluing or even taping, so the new floor bounced around while I drove.

And then came the blue. When I got the car it was numerous colours, some applied by brushes. I went to a garage where I could spray on one colour: blue.

I taped up the chrome and put newspaper over the windows, but no way was I going to wear a paper cover over my nose and mouth. I didn't want to look like a sissy. So I sprayed and sprayed some more and I did some breathing while I was spraying. All in a closed garage.

When I was done I was proud. I opened the door and showed it to the first person who passed by.

He laughed. I was hurt.

"It's a good job!" I said with emphasis.

He was looking me straight in the eyes while I was talking and he started laughing some more. Then he left.

I looked in a paint-splattered mirror in their paint-splattered bathroom and you know what I saw. Anyone with any smarts at all knows what I saw.

You don't spray without a paper mask over your nose. I had two blue streams that rose from my chin getting thicker and thicker over my lips until they streaked up like rivers into each nostril.

I coughed up blue for quite a while after that.

A few months later I sold my classic '57 Chevy for $150 and after that I drove a regular car that I forgot about, but as for the plaque on my friend's wall, no thank you. It wasn't the right shade of blue.

The Christmas Card

Ed asked us what should he do with the card?

"What do you usually do?" we answered.

"I put it under the tree. We used to have a real tree."

He was standing next to a small, very small, artificial tree with lights and decorations already on it. The tree was on a small table in their living room. Nothing else in the room said Christmas.

"Well, put it under the tree," I said.

And he did.

It was smaller than today's cards and it was simpler. On the front was a drawing of Santa's face with a beard, of course, and a cap.

And there was a funny saying, the kind one guy with no extra money would send to his friend with no extra money:

"Merry Christmas. It's kind of old and ragged
and in spots it's pretty thin. You can see it's used . . ."

The saying on the card was just the kind of thing a guy would send to another. And when you opened it:

"But *shucks*, it's good enough to use again!"

It was back in 1951 that Ed sent it to his friend Bill. They were both eighteen, both raised in the small town of Cupar, Saskatchewan, and they were both Boy Scouts.

Later that year Ed joined the Mounties. The next year Bill sent back the same card. He wrote a short note inside. That was in 1952.

The next year it went back again, Ed to Bill. The next year Bill to Ed and the next year and the next year, but in that year, 1956, Ed married Gaile so the card was signed, "Love, Ed and Gaile."

The next year Bill married Pat and the card was signed, "Love, Bill and Pat."

For the next endless years the card went back and forth, Bill and Pat, then Ed and Gaile.

Each time, a note was written inside. "Nothing new." "Going on a cruise." "New baby." And back and forth. "Baby is big." "Went to Barbados." "Kids moving out." And back and forth. Eventually the card was filled and a page was added. "Went to Expo 86." "Son married." "Stillborn daughter (cord around the neck.)" And back and forth.

Another page. "What happened to '88?" "40th anniversary." "Went to China."

And back again, filling the backs of the added pages. "Friend passed away." "Friend's daughter got her PhD." "50th anniversary."

And forth again. "Friend's mom passed away." "Another grand-daughter." "Another grandson."

Ed was a cop. Bill was involved with the John Howard Society. They said Ed caught the bad guys and sent them to jail and Bill would get them out and start them on the road to recovery.

In 2008 when they met up, the men asked that when one of

them was gone their wives would continue the card, and that they would do so until there was only one member of the foursome left.

"Can we see the card?" I asked Ed before he put it on the table under the tree. He had received it a few days earlier.

It said, "Have a wonderful Christmas, Love, Pat"

It was better than all the family albums, family trees and family stories that have ever been viewed, researched or told. And this year it is again in the mail. When we left it was the only thing under the tree. Nothing else was needed.

Hey, Cabbie

$\mathcal{K}$im, the editor with the totally adorable two-year-old whose picture is on her computer and in other photos on her walls, said, "He is very good-looking."

As a guy I find this . . . terrible. Girls and women aren't the only ones who get jealous.

I was showing her a picture in a book of Handsome Harry Hooper, a taxi driver from the early 1900s about whom I was going to do a story for a future day.

Almost always what we find during the day is what is on the air that night, but this day I remembered a story about Handsome Harry and I love Vancouver history, so there. A tale devised ahead of time.

The picture was of Harry leaning back in his cab in 1923. He has a smile. I don't know if he is handsome or not. He is a taxi driver who became a man about town, spent time in prison, was later a gold prospector and an actor and died poor. That's what I cared about, his life, not his looks.

"Not bad at all," said Kim.

I have never understood what makes a man good-looking. Other than not having a belly hanging too far over his belt, what else is there? Women see things differently.

Kim and I went on to edit the story for that day, a story of two men throwing a flying disc about the length of a football field. It wasn't a Frisbee but a wheel with a hole in the middle.

The men were amazing. They have played this game for twenty years. The object is to get the other one to drop the flying wheel. That's what boys and men do. Girls don't understand that.

That is the problem through much of life. Boys want to win. That's it. That's all. Give us a flying disc game or a war. Same thing.

Girls also want to win but from what I have seen they also want to live with the winner and comfort the loser. I read that in a book about how we evolved. Women want a winner for the sake of their children. At the same time they comfort those who fall off the swings, who usually are their children. Women have more than a tough job—it is all but impossible. Men are different: "Ha, you dropped the disc. I win."

Maybe I am entirely wrong and a throwback to a past and forgotten generation, but in any case, for those heading out in life: good luck.

Back to Handsome Harry Hooper. To do the story I needed to get the picture of him out of the book. Half the problem is solved because I wrote that book. Super, but I have to get a picture from it into a camera so it can then go through the editing computers and then be put on television. It was much simpler when our ancestors drew pictures on the walls of caves.

Kim and I finished the disc-throwing story with video of a great, tumbling, impossible catch by one of the guys; something he could tell his grandkids about.

The next day I was working with cameraman Gary Barndt and asked if he would take a picture from a book. Of course, he said, but we should find a story for today first. The story about Harry was for another day.

We go here and there, but the short of it is we go to Granville Island and as soon as we cross the wooden bridge I think: "There are turtles in that pond under the bridge." If they are awake after sleeping all winter we can get some pictures, we talk to some people and, presto, today is done.

Turtles are amazing, like most things. They take a deep breath in the late autumn, swim down to the bottom of a pond and bury themselves in the mud and muck, then close their eyes and dream.

I don't know how they do it. That is when humans would have nightmares, but turtles hold their breath for six months. Even bears when they hibernate keep breathing. But not turtles.

When it gets warmer, they throw off the blankets, swim up and take a breath. That's amazing.

Gary's education in camera work was much the same—totally amazing. When he was in BCIT there was a crisis at one of the television stations in the city. One of their cameramen had been stopped, ticketed and punished for drinking and driving. Whoops.

The plea that he could not work without driving didn't work, as it shouldn't have. He was, and is, a super guy and a super photographer but now he was super stuck. He couldn't walk to his assignments.

The powers that were in the newsroom hired two students in the journalism class to drive him around. One was Gary, the other Pete Cline, who shot the story I told you about the two veterans and the garden and the other one about the swimmer in winter.

While they missed school they got the best training. Again, even though he is at another unnamed TV station, the cameraman without the licence was one of the best cameramen in the city. Gary and Pete would drive him here and there and watch him work. There is no better way to learn. Sometimes he would let them do his work, which was good of him, or perhaps he just wanted to work less.

Gary and Pete learned from him and turned out to be as good as the fellow who had taken one sip too many. Of course, no one does anything like that anymore.

Gary and I watched some of the first turtles of spring come out of the water and struggle up on a rock. We saw a little girl named Olive and her babysitter, Kirsten, and Kirsten's daughter, Lea, looking at the turtles.

I talked to the kids and they were sweet. And there was the story: kids seeing life. Then Olive, who was about six, walked off with their carriage while Kirsten and Lea were still looking at the turtles. What could be better? A kid who had just seen turtles who carry their homes on their back now was pushing her own home on wheels.

Okay, it's a bit of a stretch but it works for television, which is very forgiving. Just look at some of the shows of superheroes and tell me where your level of disbelief kicks in. At the five-minute mark?

Anyway, Gary and I were finished, he was about to pack up and would be ready to take a picture for me from the book as soon as we got back to his truck when he turned around to wave goodbye to the parting kids and then ... It is hard to describe this, but his fifty-thousand-dollar camera sitting on a tripod so he could get close-up pictures of the turtle's head started giving into gravity and tilted forward, just a bit, then a bit more and in a slow-motion blink it leaned over past the point of no forgiveness and—plunk. It went into the pond.

It was unbelievable because you don't want to believe this is happening, the slow-motion sliding of an immensely expensive piece of machinery slipping into the stillness of cold water over which baby ducks are swimming and next to which two turtles are sitting on a rock, watching.

It was kind of funny that Gary had put a rain jacket on his camera because it looked like rain and it is important not to let the camera get wet. I could see the rain jacket being swallowed by the pond. Rain jackets are not made for use underwater.

Gary is a large man, but now he moved like a slender gymnast. He jumped down the embankment, shoved his arm into the water, grabbed one leg of the tripod and lifted it up and out all in one motion.

The turtles didn't have time to blink. The water came flooding off the camera and out from under the rain jacket, cascading down over Gary's arm and back into the pond.

Then the most important thing of all happened. There was no cursing. There was no swearing or groaning or shouting or moaning.

He pulled off the battery, which was something I would not have thought of doing, and popped out the video disc. You can tell who is a good person when there is a crisis. He stopped the circuits from shorting out any more than they already had, and he saved the reason for us being there.

"Terrible," I said.

"It'll be all right," he said. "I'll bring it back to the engineers and they'll take it apart and dry it."

"Aren't you worried?"

"Things happen," he said.

And there I saw a very fine, strong individual. I can only imagine most other people I have known going into a rage of anger or worry. Gary did nothing—except one thing.

Right after he called his boss and the engineers to let them know he was bringing in a casualty, he sent a text. It was to all the other camera folks telling them what happened.

"That will cut off the snide remarks if they hear it from someone else."

We had a lovely drive back to the television station and the pictures were beautiful, especially the close-up of the turtle's head that he had used the tripod to get. That was what the story ended with.

I don't know if Gary learned patience or forgiveness or understanding or self-control after driving around another camera guy who had once been too drunk to drive, or if he was simply born with some good genes, but anyone who can meet with triumph and disaster and treat those two impostors just the same is a neat guy. (And if you don't know about that line, please look up the poem "If" by Rudyard Kipling. It is a good lesson.)

PS: Later Gary used a spare camera and took the picture of Handsome Harry to be used in that story, and that story was fine.

I couldn't help wondering how Harry would have reacted if the seats in his cab had got soaked in a storm. Somehow that information, which we will never know, would be more important than how he looked.

Shadows

$\mathcal{I}$t was like Peter Pan, only it wasn't in the movie.

The playground was the world and the shadows were real. Peter Pan was different. He lost his shadow when he sneaked into Wendy's bedroom and she locked it in a drawer. That was to protect it, not to put it in jail. She was a good girl.

But in the playground the shadows could not get away from the kids and the kids could not get away from those controllable puppets of themselves. And that was what made it so magical.

They were jumping up and down, as they do when they are young, before school, before they have to sit in seats and listen, before they are told to be quiet. My heavens! I am sounding like Peter Pan and realizing why he didn't want to grow up.

The kids were jumping and looking at their shadows jump with them, and we got there during the meeting of kids and shadows. Lucky us. The us is camera guy Randy Raimondo and me. Randy has never been married. He plays golf. He goes on vacation to Palm

Springs with friends and mostly plays golf. He has never had kids or lived with them or played with shadows. He likes golf.

That could qualify him as a terrible grown-up, someone Peter Pan would hide from, but Randy is different. "Shadows? Sure we can do that."

After permission, of course, from the parent who is babysitting several kids along with her own, Randy puts his camera on his shoulder.

"Watch my shadow!" That was one kid standing on a small ledge and waving her arms with the sun behind her.

"No, watch mine," said another kid jumping and making his shadow do the same.

Except that when Randy came up behind them, because he is very tall and could see over the tops of their heads, his shadow overshadowed their shadows.

"Hey, your shadow is in my way," said one kid.

Randy stepped back, but now the top half of his shadow was blocking out the bottom half of theirs.

"Hey!!" they all said together, which really means *"HEY!!"* and you know what that means. Randy understood because he has heard that same thing on the golf course when someone doesn't look where they are going and kicks someone else's ball.

So Randy stood alongside them, which was good for a few shots while they made birds with flapping wings and hula dancers, but pictures on television need numerous angles or the viewers will say, "Hey, I just saw that shot. Can't you give me something new."

So Randy walked around to the top of their shadows, facing them, and took some pictures. But now shadows of the ones jumping up and down were jumping down and up, which the poor human brain, especially while watching television, cannot compute.

"Hey, what are they doing to us? Somebody call the CRTC."

The problem and the blessing was it was autumn and the sun was low. The kids' shadows were wonderful. Getting pictures of the shadows was not, but Randy got one, at just a slight angle, and another at just a slightly different angle and then of course pictures of their faces talking about their shadows and pictures of their arms waving without shadows.

And then the kids got tired of shadows and ran to the swings. Life happens that way.

After work Randy went to the golf course. His shadow went with him. Peter Pan had a good day.

The Conductor, the Traffic Cop, the Puppeteer, the Organizer, the Coach, the Ringmaster and the Central Part of Everything

She is not one of those, at least not a single one, but only because she is all of those—and more.

We are back to television news. Sorry, but that is where I make my living. And sorry because when someone tells you about someone you don't know and can't see your mind drifts. I know mine does. A friend was telling me about neighbours who used to live near him. I have no idea who they are. He is talking and I am daydreaming. But this is different.

Her name: Tanya Boguski. She is always smiling, probably to hide the insanity. She has the only job in the entire industry not taught in journalism school, mainly because students would say, "Are you kidding? That's got nothing to do with news. I'm signing up for chemistry."

Wrong. It is the most important thing in news, at least in the television variety.

To Tanya's left is the assignment editor, Scott Bills, who is from Australia, so you know everyone likes him, except the reporters who are getting assigned to stories they don't like, despite Scott's winning accent.

Reporter: "What!? That would take two days to get the information."

Scott: "Well, you have two hours."

Tanya and Scott are sitting at a long desk with three others, all of whom are either on a computer or on the phone or usually on both non-stop for eight hours, after which they are replaced by others who do the same.

All except Tanya are gathering information that may be turned into news for shows that barely take a breath before a new one is on.

Around the world all the news on television has one unifying component. Guess what that is?

Right. You are very smart. Pictures. And getting the pictures are people with cameras. That part is easy.

Scott: "Tanya, can you get a camera to Main and Hastings? There's been a stabbing."

Scott: "Tanya, can you get a camera to Oak and 16th? Terrible accident."

Scott: "Tanya, can you get a camera to City Hall. Something about something important."

Scott: "Tanya . . ."

Scott: "Tanya . . .."

Scott: "Tanya . . ."

Tanya to Scott: "Okay." "Okay." "Hard to do." "Try." "Can't be done." "Impossible." "Okay."

That is in the first ten minutes of her shift, and that is not an exaggeration. She is the camera coordinator, a terribly boring title for a heart-stopping job.

In the field, getting phone calls and texts, are the camera people. "What?" "Yes." "What?!" "Are you kidding?" "Sure."

Move one person here and another there and yet another there to fill in for that one who has a family emergency and would not leave Tanya stuck unless it was a true, extreme emergency.

This is where Tanya is also a chess player, one with a deadline. Okay, it is speed chess. And those whose days and work and lives she controls adore her.

When it is raining, the camera people are in the rain; when it is cold they are in the cold; when it is impossible to be where they must be they are in Tanya's hands.

She simply says to those inside, who are out of the rain and cold, who want it done *now*, she says: "No." News is everything but it's not more than the camera people who get directed by her.

Never, ever have I seen her ask or heard of her asking them to do something that cannot be done—and never have they said no if she asks.

She also knows basically the entire geography of the city. "Go to Main and 12th. It's on the corner with the building that has the cinder blocks with bumps."

"Victoria and Charles. Next to the tiny park."

She said her father would drive the family around the city when she was small. He loved the place. She does too.

I have seen many do this totally thankless and non-stop job. The bad ones end with bad television shows. The good ones make good ratings.

As you may have guessed, this is simply a tribute to someone who does her job so well that others will do anything for her. The bottom line to administrators everywhere: If you want your people to be good, be good to them.

Spend a day watching Tanya. Be good and you will get it back. Stand up for your people and you will get everything in return. That should be a lesson in every school.

Amen.

Lemonade Stand

This will be short, but it is one of those things that makes me believe in a spiritual something somewhere that cannot be denied no matter how much you say that it had nothing to do with it.

So, again, don't argue.

Yesterday, April 17, 2016, my wife and I had dinner with some friends who live in a warm and wonderful part of the city. It is the vast West Side. Doesn't matter if you have no idea where that is. Just think of some nice place.

There were five couples. We had some appetizers and some wine. Then the women wanted to take a walk, with their wine, which is technically illegal. How stupid is that?

I had a choice. Stay with the men or walk with the women. Are you kidding? I don't care how much kidding I get, women win, always. Especially when they are walking with wine, even if it is against the law.

We walked. We sipped. We, mostly they, talked about how pretty some houses were and how sad it was that some old ones had been pulled down to make a hole in the ground for a new super house to rise up from.

My heart is hard on this matter. I hate to see the old beauties die, but change is part of life. The original Rome was knocked down and a new one put on top of it. Then that was knocked down and on top of that a new one. It has happened many times. Someday a tour guide will take visitors in the tunnels below the towers of Vancouver.

"These were called houses. People lived in them. They were separated from other houses by grass that was eaten by crows looking for larvae that came from eggs that were laid by beetles. People got sick of seeing their grass torn up so they moved into condos. In short, it was the beetles that brought about the end of home ownership in the city."

But not yet in the West Side. They still have houses and they are on quiet streets that are named after trees. There is Arbutus and Balsam and others. And while walking we saw some boys at a lemonade stand. This is wonderful, super and everything else.

First, it is there. It is not something I am wishing for, it is really there in front of us. I am always amazed by the sight of anything that might turn into something amazing. And they were boys. Usually girls have lemonade stands, so this is better than ever.

What's more, they are polite and friendly and smiling.

The only problem was, it was *Sunday* and I wasn't working.

"Will you be here tomorrow?" I asked knowing they would say no.

"Yes," they said. A Pro-D Day. What the heck is that? I know what it is but, honestly, teachers didn't have them when I went to school so there is no need for them now. But thank you for having one tomorrow.

"Will you be here about eleven thirty?" I asked, because that would fit into my schedule, which of course is very important to me.

"We sleep until noon," said one of them.

"What?" I said.

"We aren't going to school."

Okay, I understand, but for someone who has gotten up before six every morning for most of my life I don't understand noon. Noon is for lunch.

I told them if they were there at eleven thirty they would be on television. They were excited.

The women and I walked back to our party. A block away I looked up at the street sign. Vine. I knew it was 14th Avenue, and I could remember one before Vine. They are all alphabetical so it should be easy. And then we rejoined the party and I had a little more wine. That was yesterday.

Now, jump ahead to this morning. I meet cameraman Gary Rutherford at 10:45. He tells me about the party he went to the night before. They had good wine. I do not get into comparisons because the host at the party I went to almost lives for wine, good wine. Wine is like love. You cannot compare it the next day without bragging or sounding stupid.

"Vine and 14th," I say. "Lemonade stand." It is better than saying, "Main and Hastings, dead guy."

We get there and the corner is empty. Sad. I told Gary about how good the kids were and how it would make a nice story and how I thought they would like to be on television and how I wanted them to be there.

But no one. Sad, for them and me.

"We will find something else in this neighbourhood," Gary said.

This isn't optimism. This is because it has taken a while to get here and we can't waste the time driving somewhere else to start over.

We go two blocks and see a lawn completely surrounded with strips of white cloth tied to strings attached to posts. Nice. But not that unusual.

Then two houses away from that we see a lawn covered with pinwheels, colourful and spinning. Remember, anything moving is good on television. So there are rags on one side and pinwheels on the other.

I knock on the door with the rags. No answer. I knock on the door with the pinwheels. No answer. This is what real estate agents, people collecting for Greenpeace and Jehovah's Witnesses go through every day. Don't envy them.

Between them both is a house with nothing flapping, flying or spinning. No protection. Just a lawn and a house.

Gary says, "It's about the woman in the middle."

Brilliant, I think. "Okay," I say.

She too doesn't answer the door but we can hear some clipping in the back. This is a very quiet neighbourhood.

We go around to the back lane.

"Hello, don't want to bother you."

I tell her where we are from, what we do, how we do it and why we do it.

I tell her that her neighbours have much bird protection but she is different.

"Is there something wrong with that?" she asks. She sounds defensive.

"No. We just want to take a picture and talk to you about it."

She says she will think about it. She doesn't sound enthused. Actually, she sounds annoyed. This is not a problem. Anyone is allowed to sound any way they like, especially when talking to someone in a back lane.

But she says she will see us at the front.

Gary and I go back to the front. He takes pictures of the woman's yard and the other two next door. It is a stunning contrast. Two overdone and one non-done.

We wait and wait—and we do more of the same. Gary says she is probably combing her hair. We wait. She didn't look like she had that much hair.

I am feeling bad, of course. The lemonade kids didn't show up and now the woman with the lawn free of bird-scaring devices doesn't show up.

We wait a little longer and then quit. You can't make someone do something they don't want to do. I am sad.

Okay, we turn around and take one more look for the kids, whom I really want to put on television.

We drive by 14th and Vine. No kids, but then Gary turns his head to watch for traffic coming the other way and says, "There's something at the end of the street."

He turns. He drives. Almost invisible, past the trees, past the parked cars, we see the kids. Happiness is a lemonade stand.

It is on the corner of 14th and Yew. One block away from Vine. Of course! Now I remember. How could I forget? When I told myself 14th and Vine I also told myself the kids were one block away from Vine.

The kids had been waiting for an hour.

The story was so much better than just a lemonade stand. First they had a secret ingredient. One cap of lime water in a pitcher of lemon and water and sugar. That made all the difference.

And one of the kids had made the signs and he wanted to be a cartoonist. He was twelve.

But most of all, they were giving half their money to BC Children's Hospital. When we saw them they had already made two dollars. One of them would go to charity.

It was the best lemonade stand ever, but if the woman living between the rags on one side and the pinwheels on the other had come out we would have done something with her. I don't think it would have been very good but we try to do something with everything we get. There would have been something there, I would have kept saying to myself, and when we'd finished we would have driven away. And since Gary's truck was parked facing away from where the kids were we wouldn't have seen them. And since it was getting late we wouldn't have checked again. It was only because the woman didn't walk around to the front of her house we went back for the kids.

You tell me, but I know the answer: the story god is not going to miss out on a cup of lemonade, especially one with a secret ingredient.

Private Parking

It should not have been that hard to find. You could have done it. You would have walked up and down a few blocks and said, "There! See? Just like I told you. It wasn't that hard."

Yes it was.

For fifteen years I told people about the Cadillac buried in a front yard. It was sort of nose down at an angle like it had fallen out of the sky. Just its back half was sticking up out of the ground. You can't miss it.

The first time we saw it was on an aimless cruise through some of the beautiful side streets of Kitsilano. That was somewhere between Broadway and the beach, which goes on forever and is something nice to have in a neighbourhood.

"Wooohh. Is that a Cadillac we see sticking up out of that front garden?"

Yes it was and, wow, it was a wonderful story. Tell me, how many Caddies have you seen growing next to tulips just off a sidewalk?

Okay, you have lived a more exciting life than me.

Knock, knock. This was a decade and a half ago. And out of the house behind the car came a happy fellow. Steve Edmundson. Wiry, with hippie long hair, and pouring out energy. He had bought the car to take parts out of it to restore another Caddy, both of them built in 1960, but by the time he had finished the project he had grown fond of the car that was sacrificing its carburetor and drive shaft so that another could live.

"I wasn't going to send it to the junkyard. Sad, that would be. So I cut off the front and let the back half stand up in the front yard, like it had fallen from the sky."

That's what he said the first time I met him. I can quote him because I remember it because you don't forget things like that.

In his backyard he also had the front of a motorcycle standing up like it had just come screaming out of Hades and got stuck halfway to heaven. The bike had high-rise handlebars so you know it was not a polite weekend cruiser kind of guy who had been riding it.

But in the middle of his yard he had the most wonderful thing of all. It was a hot day and Steve said, "Check out that tunnel."

It was a box, a long box with an open front and open back. It was tall enough to walk through. It smelled so good.

I walked in and sniffed. The heaven the motorcycle was headed for was right here, a few steps away from the high-rise bars. It was wisteria that had been trained to go up and over to the other side, and it was more wisteria on the other side that had been trained to do the same.

There was a metal frame that it grew on because wisteria will win out over everything except steel.

As a side note, we once lived in a wonderful old house. It was built in 1910 and in the front it had had a round balcony open to the air but covered from the rain. It was no longer there when we moved in. What we saw was a 1960s replacement that was square and functional. It kept off the rain but it was not elegant.

Much later I saw a photo from 1910 or 1920. There were young girls posing on the round balcony, possibly for a birthday party.

Around them on the wooden frame of their photo setting were the thick vines of wisteria. Hanging from the vines were the flowers that smell so good. Being pulled down by the vines was the balcony. In time the dead wood gave in to the living wood and the balcony was no more.

We had the nice square balcony, with no wisteria.

But it sure smells so good, and it was so cool when we went into the tunnel that Steve with the Cadillac had made. A picnic table was in the middle with plenty of room to get on and off the bench seats.

Cool and fragrant. Wow.

Years later I wanted to show my wife but I couldn't remember where it was. I wanted to show many others, at least the Cadillac, but the same. Where the heck did I see it? Ever lose your keys? I lost a Cadillac.

The story I'd done had no location other than Kitsilano. How dumb can anyone get?

The years passed. It's here, somewhere. Or there. Or the next street. But I couldn't find it.

Then, fifteen years later, I was wandering around the area with Murray the Camera Guy, that would be Murray Titus, as you read earlier. He was driving west on Broadway.

"Nothing here," I said. Broadway is boring. Around the Cambie area are big buildings and if you don't have a tag hanging around your neck with the right bar code on it you can't get past the front doors.

Farther west are the small shops. The folks in those work seven days a week. They are good and nice and kind but they don't have time to tell a visitor about the birthday party for their goldfish, if they had a goldfish.

Murray turns right, going to the beach. That's nice, so nice that I have done hundreds of stories on the beach at Kitsilano, so if you get bored, go there. You will find something neat.

"Can't go there," I said. "Been there too many times."

Then I added, just from a flickering thought in the left-hand corner of my mind, "Would you drive along 6th Avenue? I once saw a Cadillac buried in a front yard."

Murray is the same guy who often hears on his phone, "Would you go to (a location). There's a dead guy in the street."

Murray drives and I have no hope, and then—you know what I'm going to say—and then *there it is.* "Hey, that's a Cadillac buried in a front yard," he said.

I'm glad he saw it first. There is nothing like discovering something for yourself. Socrates knew that. If you don't know who I am talking about, look up Socrates. He was the best teacher who ever lived. He never taught anything. He only asked questions of his students and they discovered the answers. In short, they taught themselves.

Plato was one of his students. Look up his name while you're at it.

"That's really a Cadillac in the front yard," Murray repeated, because for really good things you have to say them twice.

"Please be home." That was me praying.

The back of a Cadillac sticking out of the ground in a front yard is no good if no one is there to tell you about it. If you are just passing by and take a picture it doesn't matter but can you imagine what the lack of a person would be like on television?

"Here is the back of a Cadillac," would say the news anchor. "It is sticking out of the ground." You see the picture. "And now the weather."

"Please be home."

I knock and a young fellow opens the door. The young fellow was a five-year-old when I last saw him. He doesn't remember me. Duh.

"My father is still sleeping. I'll get him."

No kidding. And thank you.

Steve comes out, slim, wiry, pouring out energy and putting a cowboy hat over his hippie long hair.

He hasn't changed. None of us ever do unless we want to.

He is happy to see me. I am happier to see him.

The same story, he loved the car and kept it. But what to do with it? Same story. Stick it in the front yard.

"Look at the licence plate," Steve says.

I don't remember this from the first visit.

CME 007. When he buried the car everyone knew what 007 meant. But Steve was pointing to the letters "Those are my son's initials. Colin Morgan Edmundson."

"Growing up here was strange," said Colin Morgan Edmundson. He didn't have to explain.

The motorcycle and cool tunnel were gone, he said. That proves I was wrong about wisteria. It can take down steel. And once that was gone there was no heaven for the hog to shoot for. So it was gone too.

Then Steve said he tells kids in the neighbourhood that his car fell from the sky. Most believe him. I do too.

When we left, Murray the Camera Guy said he wanted his sweetheart to see it. So for his sake I will remind him it is at 6th Avenue and Balaclava Street.

Of course I know he would never forget.

If you get a chance, go by too, and tell your kids there is only one way it could have gotten there, just like Steve said.

Chocolate Chip Cookies

There is nothing better. Period.

When I was young we had Chips Ahoy. They were the best. When my kids were young they had Chips Ahoy. They were still the best.

Then I started fooling around in the kitchen. Lord! What you can do with no experience, no training and no one telling you that you need experience and training, as well as a recipe. You can do better than Chips Ahoy, at least in my humble opinion.

I had no recipe. I just figured I know what's in cookies. I have read the ingredients on cookie packages and if you leave out the chemicals it is fairly simple.

This will be short because there isn't much to it, except the wow factor.

A large hunk of butter, more or less. *Never* margarine, because butter tastes better. That's all. If you read everything on the internet on what's good about butter or what's good about margarine you will go blind.

I grew up with margarine and according to contemporary medical advice I am surprised I am still alive. Everyone ate margarine because there was a war and butter was going for the fighting men. After being in uniform myself I bet it went for the officers.

We had margarine that came with packets of yellow colouring. Can you just imagine what was in those? The margarine was white but to pretend it was butter you mixed in the chemical concoction. This was the age when a major industrial producer's slogan was, "Better Living Through Chemistry." Sounds good.

And, by the way, margarine came to you white because the dairy farmers of America didn't want the competition so they lobbied the law makers to have it look like lard, which does not look good.

The margarine makers added the packets of yellow dye, which the housewife—sorry to say that but the word came from an age in early human evolution—tipped into the margarine and then stirred. Some of the margarine came out deep yellow, some light, some white and some striped. Bon appétit!

We put margarine on everything. Margarine used to contain trans fat. I have read about it but I don't know what it is. We are told it causes heart disease, hard arteries and bad dreams. We used it every day. I think this proves that contemporary medical advice is valuable to those who sell it.

Now I use butter, so put in half a pound. What is half a pound? Buy a hunk of butter at the supermarket and cut it in half. That's good enough, and that's the only measurement.

Then pour some sugar over it. How much? Good question. Answer? A lot. Just cover the hunk of butter until you can't see it and that's about right.

Then stick in your hands. This is the best part. Grab that butter and sugar and squeeze. Then squeeze it again.

Someone will say, "You should use an electric all-purpose blender."

Tell them to go away. This is caveman cookie-making.

If you want the cookies to look dark use brown sugar. If you don't care and don't want to spend the extra for brown sugar use white. It's all sweet.

Did you know that basically half the trade in human lives that was called the slave trade was because of sugar? In the early days the only sweetener in Europe was honey. Then someone said this granulated stuff that looks like sand and comes from tall, thick grasses that grow mostly in the Caribbean tastes unbelievably good.

Bang. Capture and import millions of poor souls from Africa and ship them in chains to the West Indies to cut sugar cane. That was a larger and more brutal slavery than anything in the US.

First, burn the cane fields to get rid of the leaves off the stalks. Then send the slaves out to cut and carry. Life expectancy was two years. During the first two days they wished they would die, but Europe got its white sugar and rotten teeth.

Back to the cookies. Amazing how unbearably bitter information mixes with an irresistibly sweet conclusion. Such is the human condition. No slaves now, but please, brush your teeth after a cookie.

Squeeze and kneed the butter and sugar until the sugar is gone. This is a trick of nature, fat hides sweetness but it becomes fatter. That is a lesson you see every day.

Then put in a capful of vanilla. I don't know why but my mother used it so I do.

And then an egg. The mixture will now be sticky and gunky on your hands. Such is life. Stick with it. It will turn out warm and good.

Then some salt. How much? Too much is terrible. Too little is tasteless. Face it, salt is what sells KFC and fries and potato chips. We aren't talking healthy, we are talking tasty. Put in a little extra, but not too much. If you worry about your blood pressure, walk around the block. That's better than worrying about a quarter teaspoon of anything.

Then oatmeal. Oatmeal is the best thing in the world. I've had few days in my adult life pass without oatmeal. It doesn't matter if it is slow cooking or instant, oatmeal is good for you.

By the way, did you know that someone judged those words,

". . . is good for you," as the best advertising slogan ever in the English-speaking western world. Except it was Guinness's beer that used it. Guinness Is Good for You. Actually, Guinness *is* good for you, like all beer and wine, *if* you drink only a little.

Small chance of that happening.

In case you are interested, the second-best advertising slogan ever written was Drink Coca-Cola. In two words it told you what to do, when to do it and what to do it with. The only problem with Coke is that it isn't good for you, although their early promotions said it cured every ailment you could dream of.

It's a bit like the modern advertisements for drugs on television. "Take X drug and it will cure your erectile dysfunction, your hair loss and your bad breath."

And while you are watching the commercial with lovely young people with full heads of hair and obviously good breath and are so close you know they have no problem with ED, you hear, or barely hear, that this drug may also cause heart attacks, strokes, liver disease, thoughts of suicide, bad chequebook balancing and early death. You are watching the couple getting closer together, smiling, cooing, smiling some more, cooing some more and you know what is going to happen if they don't have liver disease or commit suicide before it happens.

So you buy the drug.

The same with Coke. On the commercials you see smiling young people tilting back the ice-cold bottles. I would smile too if only I had one of those.

Back to oatmeal. It is good for you, so pour in a bunch. Then some more. You can't go wrong. Horses like it.

With your fingers squeeze the oatmeal into the butter and sugar. This is another trick of nature. Fat makes even good stuff disappear but it doesn't work the other way round. If you want to get rid of fat you have to get rid of fat. You can't add more stuff to it and hope it goes away.

Anyway, when the oatmeal has disappeared into the butter, put in some flour. Not too much. You have to also squeeze that into the goop of butter and sugar and oatmeal and salt and egg. So squeeze some more. Pretend you are in a glue factory. There's no way around it, it is sticky.

Then add baking powder. Baking *soda* is different. Everyone uses baking soda for almost everything and it is good for almost everything. You can wash just about anything from your body to your car tires with it. It is the duct tape of cleaning.

But don't use it for cookies because it tastes like salt and you already have real salt in the cookies.

So I put some baking powder in my hand. About that much. Too much isn't bad—your cookies will be fatter. Too little is okay, too. The cookies will be thinner, unlike you and me after eating them.

And then the chocolate chips. Lots of them. Doesn't matter what brand. Pay a lot or a little. They are like wine—after the first mouthful the cheaper ones taste fine. Squeeze them in.

And you can figure out the rest. Make little cookies, bake them at 350F or 180C for ten minutes and, presto, in less time than it took you to read all this—cookies!

Or buy Chips Ahoy and you'll still have a happy crowd.

The Lady and the Cookies

She is old. She will be ninety-seven when you are reading this. Much of the world has changed since she started out.

My wife and I take her out for coffee and cookies every week. We started out by driving her to a park where she walked around and watched the kiddies play. She could watch them for a long time, smiling all the while.

Now she is in a wheelchair. We push her to a coffee shop when the weather is nice. Last week I made some of the cookies that you've just read about. She likes them.

Outside in the sunshine she ate and drank and then along came a girl with orange socks that went up to her shorts.

The sweet little old lady poked me to make sure I didn't miss this. She smiled and shook her head, which means, "Why?"

"There are new styles now," I said.

Then along came a girl with green hair.

"Look," said the sweet little old lady.

"Don't point," said my wife. "It's not polite."

"But look," said the sweet little old lady. "Why did she do that?"

"It's the way kids do things now," I said.

One time, when we could take her on longer trips, we were pushing her past a resort hotel and there was a wedding in progress on the front lawn.

There were two women standing side by side.

"Where's the mister?" asked the sweet little old lady.

"There is none," we told her. "Sometimes women marry women and men marry men."

"Why?"

"Well, that's the way things are now," I said.

We kept walking and pushing and her head kept turning back like an owl, a wise old owl who still had things to learn.

But last week was the best. We were sitting outside a coffee shop in a small shopping plaza and she was eating my cookies. She nodded when she took the first bite, which means they were okay, the same as they have always been. They are a constant in her life.

Then a Winnebago pulled into the parking lot.

"That's a nice bus," she said.

"That's a private bus," we said. "Someone is going travelling."

Out of the bus came a bride, with full wedding dress, and following her were two bridesmaids with full bridesmaid's dresses.

"Is there a church here?" she asked.

They went into the coffee shop. Meanwhile one of my cookies had made it halfway to her mouth. It stayed there while she stared at the door of the coffee shop.

Then the door opened and the bride came out carrying two takeout containers followed by the bridesmaids, each carrying a container. One of the bridesmaids picked up the train of the white wedding dress and held it while they crossed the parking lot.

"Why are they doing that?" asked the sweet lady.

"They are probably celebrating with lattes," I said.

"What's a latte?"

"A very expensive way to get coffee with milk."

The wedding party with the takeouts went back to the bus and climbed in.

The little old lady took a bite of the cookie that was still in her hand.

She chewed for a minute and then said, "I like your cookies."

When we went back to the nursing home I gave her the last cookie I had. She took it and wrapped it in a napkin.

As the world changes and goes crazy, and it is always doing that, it is recommended by cookie-makers everywhere that you hold onto something sweet from the past. One bite and you understand.

Another Fish Story

They were looking over the metal railing around False Creek. There were two small boys, two parents and two grandparents. The boys and the parents were from Alberta, visiting the grandparents who were here.

"There's a fish," said one of boys. He was six.

I looked over the railing. I didn't want to intrude so I was several steps away, but I could hear them and I could look. What I saw were some bottles and a square piece of metal on the sand and gravel under the water.

"It's a square fish," the boy said.

I interrupted and asked the parents if we could talk to the boys. The grandparents said they only get to see their grandkids twice a year and this was a wonderful day.

The parents said yes, we could talk, and the boy began:

"I saw a square fish. Really I did. We have bigger fish in Alberta, but this is the first square fish I've seen."

His bigger brother, who was nine, pushed his little brother and said, "There's no such thing as a square fish. That's a piece of junk down there."

The little brother said, "No! I saw a square fish."

"Didn't."

"Did."

"Didn't."

Then grandpa came into the picture.

"I once caught a fish that I thought was square."

Little grandson looked up with a smile.

Big grandson looked up with a frown.

"But when I got it on land it was different."

Frown faded, smile held on.

"It was both fish-shaped and square."

Two faces, two question marks.

"I think there are square fish and regular fish and you can find anything you want in the ocean," said grandpa.

Two happy faces. Then little grandson ran up to grandpa's belly and with the excitement of being with grandpa bumped into the protruding round target with his head and grandpa went "Humph." And big grandson came running too but grandpa sidestepped him and big grandson missed.

"Close," said grandpa, relieved.

Then grandsons went around in a circle again and grandpa stepped to his left then his right and he was the happiest man on earth.

Somewhere under the water of False Creek a square fish was happy being recognized as the only living, breathing thing a six-year-old from Alberta had seen today, even if it was a piece of metal lying on the gravel. If you believe it is so, it is.

The Blind Gardener

It is not the ideal spot for a garden. It has car exhaust and marijuana smoke and thieves and noise and homeless kids with their dogs sitting on the sidewalk.

It has transvestites passing by and drag queens and boys holding hands with boys and girls doing the same with girls. It has torn jeans and business suits and pizza eaten on the street.

It is not a backyard home garden with peas and peace and birds, although this one does have pigeons.

This is the garden at the northwest corner of Davie and Burrard Streets. Before the garden there was a gas station, so the soil needed a bit of remediation before planting carrots, but it is a beautiful spot and you can feel good just walking past.

Look inside. Most of the plots are neat and in the spring and summer most have someone oblivious to the buses less than four steps away watering their radishes.

Wait. Wait just a second. That man, on his knees pulling up

weeds, has a dog next to him and the dog has a harness that Seeing Eye dogs carry.

The man reaches back and pets the dog and then puts one of his hands into the dirt. We move a few steps closer. He doesn't see us. Of course he doesn't. He's blind.

We can see that. We can see his hand moving around the dirt feeling for weeds. There's one. He pulls it out, then reaches back and puts it in a small pile of other weeds.

He searches again and his fingers touch another infant plant. He runs the tips of his fingers over the top then moves on.

"Excuse me. I don't want to bother you."

You know the rest of it. Then I ask and he answers:

"Yes, I am blind. Yes I garden."

He is waiting for me to ask a sensible question.

This is when there is a long pause, which I think is stupid on my part because he can hear me pausing but he can't see me going through pain while trying to ask the next question:

"How?"

That only half came out.

"I mean how do you garden. I mean, how do you know . . ."

He was very kind. He interrupted me. "It's hard to imagine, but I do it almost every day and it gets easier."

He was still on his knees. "It's okay, don't feel embarrassed. I get this all the time. The garden was planted by my brother. He's a doctor at St. Paul's."

St. Paul's Hospital is half a block away.

"I weed and water and keep it clean."

His name is Kelly.

His dog is Bonnie, a large dog. "Here, smell this." He holds some mint up to Bonnie's nose. She sneezes.

"She usually likes it," he said.

He sweeps his hand across the dirt again and says, "Darn. This is what I hate."

He holds up a cigarette butt, just the filter where the smouldering ash stopped. Someone on the sidewalk has flicked it into the garden.

"I get these all the time," said Kelly.

He doesn't add that he would like to catch someone doing it and give them a good piece of his mind but that's what I am thinking. Of course I can't say it because it would sound like, "I want to do something that you can't do." It is hard to talk to someone who doesn't fit into the traditional groove of life.

"I hate to ask, but how did you lose your sight?"

He gets up off his knees and stands. He is much taller than me and much stronger. Funny how he will probably never know that, or care.

"I was hit by a car. Kingsway near Edmonds."

That was it. He was on a crosswalk. He had the light. Someone wasn't paying attention. Someone had something else to do that was more important.

"I was in the hospital for a quite a while. I got an infection in my eyes and that was it."

He has one prosthetic eye and the other just doesn't work. That would mean one was smashed too badly to stay in his body. The other could stay and do nothing.

I don't know what happened to the driver, but my bet is nothing. I didn't ask. This was about gardening and he said, "This is great. It gets me out of my apartment almost every day and I love it."

He bent down and picked up the pile of weeds and the cigarette butt and said he had to get on his way. That's where the story ends. It's not dramatic or surprising or funny or sad the way most endings in most stories try to be. We watched him walk past the garbage cans where he dropped off the intruders in his brother's plot and then left, joining the crowd on the sidewalk.

Somehow, that was the perfect ending.

A Mother's Love

The Block Watch lady saw it happen, so you know it is a trust-worthy account.

But first I want to tell you that when I was small the wildlife we saw were mostly cockroaches, which are not cute. We learned to kill them by turning off the lights in the kitchen, waiting half a minute and then flicking the lights back on.

"Go."

And we would start smacking them—six, seven, eight—before they disappeared into the cracks in the walls or behind the pantry doors.

"I got nine," said Jimmy Lee, who was a super roach killer.

"I only killed six," said Buster, who later went into the Marines.

It was both sport and community service. The more we killed the fewer there were in the kitchen, at least for an hour.

It was good when you got the ones who were going to lay eggs, and that seemed like every third one. They had a black protrusion in the rear, so if you got one of them you really got a hundred, which was still only a tiny number.

We also fished for rats. This was not a sublime neighbourhood. We would lower a string with a hook, usually from your mother's curtain rod, into the sewer. On the end of the hook was a piece of bread or salami.

Whap, there was a tug on the line, just like real fishing. There were two choices. One was to pull it up slowly without jerking and try to get the rat to the slots in the sewer before it jumped off. The other, the dramatic way, was to yank the string as hard as you could to pull the rat up through the slots before it jumped off.

Neither way worked very well. We were always ready with a brick to knock it on the head if we got it to the street but I don't remember us ever getting the chance. Sometimes we got them up to the street but then we'd jump back because they were so big, and then they took off in a blur.

Besides that our wildlife were mostly pigeons. We once made friends with a one-legged pigeon that we called Stumpy. We would run home from school and feed it with bread and cookie crumbs that we saved from our lunches.

We knew it couldn't get much food on its own because the other pigeons would get it first, so we became attached to saving Stumpy, our friend.

After a few months he/she was gone. That ended the call of the wild.

Jump ahead some years and our family moved to British Columbia.

"Quick, look through the window," I said to our daughter.

"Ahhhhheeeee," or something like that. Raccoons are cute, but not when you see just the eyes staring at you through the kitchen window.

There are also hummingbirds, which are beyond amazing. How can anything move that fast or not move while moving so fast?

And eagles. After being almost wiped out by our love of

chemicals to control everything they have come back with soaring beauty. Sometimes I see a pair, always a pair, gliding over our home. They are so high I can barely see them and I only noticed them at first by accident. Now I can't take my eyes off them.

There are also crows. Now if you are from here you probably don't like crows, but I didn't grow up with them so I like them. So there.

What I like most is their social lives. I did a story on this once when I learned about their parties. If you live in Vancouver you see this every night. Of course if you live anywhere there are crows, but in Vancouver you can watch them blot out parts of the sky just at sunset. They are flying to Burnaby. Party town I suppose, at least for crows.

At Highway 1 and Willingdon they land on the rooftops of the industrial buildings that have businesses inside but I don't know what.

Where those buildings are there were trees not many years ago and the crows landed in them. Now they spend their nights on the rooftops. They are adapting to a changing world.

But what I learned they are doing, after I talked to some crow experts, is *partying!* Every night. Gossip, talk, visiting, yakking it up.

You see, in the spring the couples—and they do mate for life even though they cheat a lot, said the crow experts—the couple start gathering sticks and things to make a home.

Then they get together and, presto, babies in the bedroom. You know about all the work that comes with babies. No time for parties. Mom and Pop are off to the supermarket on the grass every five minutes. Boy those kids can eat.

Spring is spent with little sleep for the parents. We could have warned them.

Summer is the same, except now the worry when they go out on their own is will they be safe? Will they find a good lawn with beetles that they can dig up before the human comes out and chases them away? Will they be able to fly out of the way of cars while they are feasting on the remains of something that was slower?

So much on the minds of parents. We could have warned them about this, too.

And after that there is the other problem of getting them to move out. "Go away. You're grown up. Now go fly."

"But we like it here. If we can't find beetles or roadkill we know you will provide."

"*Go!*"

We could have told them about that, too.

But finally comes autumn. The kids are gone. The home needs so many repairs it's easier to move out. The sun no longer shines in our eyes when we're trying to sleep.

"Let's party!"

And so the sky darkens with tens of thousands of crows coming from Vancouver and Coquitlam and even Burnaby, all heading for the Highway 1 and Willingdon Night Club. Every night. No matter what the weather, these are hard-partying birds.

If you want to watch, look for MacDonald's near the Willingdon on-ramp to the highway westbound. Park by the row of buildings that look a bit like factories except they are not.

Get out of your car—and duck.

"Howard, get back in the car! The birds are attacking us!"

Swarms of crows are descending on them. (I know the official word is a murder of crows but, honestly, that is stupid to say even if they do gang up for some killings occasionally.) And actually at Highway 1 and Willingdon they are flying everywhere and it just *looks* like they are attacking Howard and Margaret. They won't really murder them.

"Margaret, it's okay. I just wanted to show you how much fun it would be to go out at night."

"In the car, Howard, this minute! I never want to come here again. And I am not going out at night ever again, not as long as these devils are out."

Okay, it's not an ideal night for everyone, but if you aren't terribly fearful of many, many black birds flying over your head and if you never saw Alfred Hitchcock's terrifying movie *The Birds* then you should be fine.

So go if you get the chance.

Now back to the start of the story, the mother's love. This is the way the Block Watch lady, Christine, saw it from her kitchen window.

A mother bear and her baby bear were crossing the street alongside our house. This is right after they took a bath in our other neighbour's backyard pond. She is Sandra and she said, "My dogs were going crazy."

She has two tiny, really, really small, dogs. They are the kind that bark at bears, which shows complete insanity or total self-confidence.

"I looked out the window and the bears were sitting in my pond. Both of them. It looked so sweet, except they were wrecking it."

Then the bears left and crossed the street to my backyard. This is where the Block Watch lady comes in.

"The mother bear climbed over your fence," Christine said. The fence is about chest high.

"But the baby bear couldn't get up. It kept trying to scratch at the fence but it didn't work. So the mother bear climbed back over and with her front leg she punched a hole through your fence. Just one punch. Big hole."

Christine is a very good Block Watch lady. She notices all the details.

"Then the mother bear went back over the top again and her baby followed her through the hole."

I felt like saying, "Ahhhhh, that's so nice," except I now had a fence with a hole in it. On the other hand the simple, practical solution to a child's needs is what every mother spends much of her life coming up with, and my fence had played a part in that.

I liked the story so much I left the hole for more than a week, in case anyone asked me about it. No one did.

"You should fix that hole; it looks terrible," my wife said.

"But it's about a mother's love," I said.

"It's a hole," said this woman who knows all about raising children and coming up with practical solutions to impossible needs.

The fence is now fixed, but I love that bear, even if I never saw it.

Charlie's Tree

$\mathcal{O}$f only he had waited a hundred years. That is not much to ask. If he had, those who run a government agency would have finally come around to his way of thinking. But no, he didn't have enough patience for that.

Charlie Perkins did what he did but if he had waited through his children's lives and grandchildren's and great-grandchildren's, things would have been fine.

It is weird how the world changes. It always amazes me how Japanese tourists go to Pearl Harbor.

I, like many of you, was born when thousands of Canadian and American and British and Australian soldiers were dying getting onto the beaches of Normandy. Germans were killing them. Now Germans vacation there, next to tourists from Canada, America, Britain and Australia.

Decades later I was a tiny part of the war effort when tens of thousands of young Americans were being killed in Vietnam. Now it's a vacation spot for young Americans looking for surf, sand and tours of the tunnels.

I don't get it. I've said this many times. Why don't we just skip the wars and take vacations.

It seems impossible now, more than impossible, but no doubt someday the children of Islamic terrorists, the ones who don't blow up themselves before having children (and dear editor, please don't take out that line to be less hurtful), will be on tours of New York and Paris oohing and aahing at the sights and history. It has to happen.

Humans are not only scary; they are crazy.

Charlie Perkins was neither. He was wonderful and brave and did what he had to do. But if only if he had waited . . . a hundred years.

I've told this story before, but now it has a new ending, the hundred-year part.

Charlie was a farmer in the Fraser Valley who came of the age for early dying when World War I started.

Canada, supporting Britain, as was its duty and right, went to war with Germany from the beginning. Charlie, like all his friends, hitched up his horse and took the long ride to Vancouver to enlist in a trip that went to hell. They didn't know that, but they did know this is what they should do, so they did it.

Charlie was bright and was sent to flying school. Airplanes were newer than electronic cars are now. Actually, that is a bad comparison. Airplanes were terrifying. Okay, they were exciting to watch, but the chances of them staying in the air were slim. Charlie was told to keep one in the air and to shoot the bad guys, which he did.

When he got back to his farm in Langley he was different. I never met Charlie, of course, but I have known others who come back after they have killed and seen others killed and they are different. All of them.

He was steadfast. If he was like most, like almost all, he didn't talk about what he had seen and done. When the subject of "What did you do in the war?" came up he said . . . long pause . . . nothing.

But one day he was in his fields, which you know so well. Yes, you do. You know the land where Charlie stood behind a horse and plowed and sweated and looked up at the sky and said, "Lord, when will this day end?"

You know the farm. I'll tell you why in a moment.

One day he said, "I should do something for the guys."

Those were the guys who were in graves in France. Some had become his best friends. Now they were in plywood coffins or just in canvas bags, under the mud in a cemetery far away.

"I should do something."

So he got a tiny baby cedar tree. It was the same as your kids get, or used to get, in school. It was about the height of half a kid's arm. Not much, but something. He planted it on a rise just off the corn field.

And it grew. It grew the size of Charlie. It grew the size of his airplanes. It grew and grew and he was happy and he put a sign on it one November 11th that said, "This is for my friends."

And a long time later . . . it is hard to say when, numbers just get in the way . . . a long time later the government of Canada was doing something wonderful. It was building a road across the country. It would be called the Trans-Canada Highway.

It was headed straight for Charlie's tree.

Now here is where political correctness and facts get confused. A long time ago I met a nephew of Charlie. He told me that when the bulldozers were coming at the tree Charlie stood in front of it with a shotgun and said: "Don't."

I did a story about that.

Then some of Charlie's grandchildren called me, very upset, and said their grandfather would never have done that. Their grandfather was law abiding.

They told me I should never say their grandfather would defy the law with a gun, especially a shotgun.

No one that we know actually saw what happened. The facts are that Charlie was in front of the tree, the bulldozers were coming and there was a stalemate: the workmen against the veteran. It was not easy or nice.

Both sides needed patience and wisdom.

To stop the progress of the highway meant high-priced delay. To change the highway for a tree was impossible. Millions of trees had already been killed for the sake of cars.

Calls were made to Phil Gaglardi. Phil was a politician you could love. He got speeding tickets on the same highways he had built. He was outgoing and outspoken. He was fun.

Much later I wanted to do a profile on him so I went to his office in Kamloops.

"No, I can't disturb him now. He's at lunch," his secretary said.

"Will he be back soon?"

"Oh, he's in there, but he won't see anyone now."

"He doesn't like to be disturbed while he's eating?" I asked.

"No, while he's naked."

Oh my gosh my golly. "What did you say?"

She looked very serious like a good government official's secretary.

"He's naked in there."

"Naked?"

She nodded, then stared back at whatever work she would otherwise be doing were she not telling someone that in the closed office her boss was naked.

I looked at the heavy wooden door, on which a sign said:

"Phil Gaglardi, MLA." With my X-ray vision I saw what she was saying so I closed my eyes and looked away.

"He feels better afterwards," she said.

In a little while, the time it takes to get on your pants and shirt and suit jacket, her intercom buzzed.

"Yes, sir," she said.

"Back from lunch," said the voice through the speaker.

"There's someone to see you," she said to the box.

"Send him in," said a voice that was friendly and happy and sounded very suit jacketish.

She opened the door.

"Hello, sir," I said, and then added, "I don't mean to be forward, but do you really run around your desk naked?"

"Every day," said MLA Gaglardi. "You should try it."

Okay, let's get on with other matters, any other matters.

He said that when he heard about Charlie and the tree he told the crew chiefs on the highway, "Well curve the road around the tree, for God's sake. That's for dead heroes." And the road was curved, around the tree, near the 200th Street exit.

And that to me was one of the world's greatest solving of engineering and humanitarian problems. I know it is not like fixing racial or religious injustice, but just think, another politician could have said, "Send it to a committee and we will study it." Gaglardi made a decision and it worked and it was good.

For the next fifty years cars went around the tree. There were a few small flags next to it and nailed into the bark was a small sign that said, "In memory of my fallen comrades." Very simple.

Except that only a few people saw it, because as you drove around the curve in the road the tree was the last thing you would see. If you were a good driver you had your eyes on the road.

"What's that?"

"What's what?"

"I saw a tree over there."

"There's lots of trees."

"But this was a tree with a something on it."

"Don't know. Didn't see it."

And the tree disappeared around the curve.

And then some rotten teenagers set fire to the tree. That killed it.

That was in the 1980s. The top half was cut off and it became even more invisible. Eventually it was covered with ivy. Go around a curve in the road and look for half a tree covered with ivy with an old, small sign on it. Not likely.

That is about the time I did the story on it and the nephew said: "Charlie had a shotgun."

And the grandchildren said, "Grandpa would never do that."

They could be right. Or not.

On such things history is written. The important part was that Charlie protested and Phil agreed. Beautiful story.

And then, a few decades later, so many people had moved into the valley and the city and everywhere that a new, improved highway was built. It is wide and straight and somehow the curve has been taken out and the tree, at least the trunk of it, hasn't been touched. Except now there is a large sign that says: "CHARLIES TREE."

It's impossible not to see it. Yes, we know there should be an apostrophe in Charlie's, but the sign doesn't have one so we don't have one. Go argue with Charlie.

And as for Charlie, it took a while but he won.

July 31, 2016. A sad update. In the early morning of today Charlie's tree toppled over and crashed down on the highway. After a century of battling road builders and cars and fires, it was defeated by a deadly combination of the ivy that covered and weakened it and a strong wind.

Maybe someone will plant another one.

Teamsters Can Do Anything
(Don't Ask Why)

Okay, ask why.

The answer is because Jimmy Hoffa may be in the East River, that ribbon of water between Manhattan and Brooklyn. He may be standing upright with his feet in a tub of concrete while his head is bobbing around like seaweed, if there was any seaweed in the East River, which there is not.

Jimmy Hoffa is the patron saint of the Teamsters—or he's the devil. If you think being for or against Donald Trump is exciting or dangerous it is nothing, *nothing*, compared to being for or against Jimmy Hoffa.

He raised a union of truck drivers to be one of the most powerful organizations in American *and* Canadian history. Teamsters were not just truckers and cab drivers but anyone and everyone who had anything to do with cars or trucks or anything close to them.

That included delivery personnel who unloaded things from trucks, and "Darn, that crate of Scotch just slipped out of my hands."

Once that happens it must be labelled "Damaged Goods," and must be disposed of.

"Luckily none of the bottles were broken, but rules are rules."

And the crate went to a nice home where it was well cared for.

But that was the old days. Nothing like that happens now. I attest, as a former Teamster myself, I swear I have never heard of a crate of Scotch or any crates of anything being dropped in the last long number of years. Honest.

I was a Teamster when I was a parking lot attendant at Idlewild airport in New York. That was before it became JFK airport. Don't ask. It was long ago.

I was given a uniform by the airport and a badge by the Teamsters. The badge went on the cap so you know what was the first thing anyone saw. The Teamsters taught their people from the head down.

"Don't take any guff from the employer," a much, much older Teamster told me on my first day. My employer was the airport, which ruled with its own iron hand while trying to combat the organized crime that was stealing everything it could get from the airplanes. It also took no guff from anyone.

And he said, "Don't take any guff from the customers," who didn't like paying the outrageous prices charged by the airport for parking.

Guff was a word then. Yes, it is a four-letter word, but those were cleaner times.

"But always remember who your brothers are."

And then he left me with a stack of tickets to give out when drivers entered and to exchange for dollars when they left.

I gave out and collected. When my shift was over the older fellow asked to see my receipts. He counted the money and then the tickets.

"Ummmm," he said. Then he started counting again.

"You can go now," he told me. "I'll take care of everything."

He just wanted to be accurate.

Jimmy Hoffa said the same thing but he went to prison because the judge didn't believe him. But that was long ago, when things like that sometimes, occasionally but not often, did happen.

And then Jimmy got out of prison because President Richard Nixon (who said, "I am not a crook," after he was accused of being one) let him out so long as he promised to be good.

Soon after that Mr. Hoffa couldn't be bad because he disappeared.

I tell you this because the Teamsters aren't like a union of bakers or musicians. They have an aura of toughness. Once upon a time I was at another television station that locked out its reporters and editors and photographers. Okay, they locked us out because we were on strike.

Regardless, we walked up and down around a camp stove keeping coffee warm. Days passed. Weeks passed. We wondered if anyone cared.

Then one day came the rumble of a very large engine and the blaring of horns. Large trucks carry more than one horn. Following the horns came a giant black tractor-trailer eighteen-wheeler that stopped right at our camp stove. On the side of the truck in letters 10 feet high was the word TEAMSTERS.

Then out of the cab stepped three men in heavy black jackets.

"Sorry it took so long. Can we be of assistance?" one said. "There are more of us, if you like."

We thanked them and offered our coffee. They in turn took out enough food to feed us through the winter, and it wasn't yet cold.

I don't know if that had anything to do with anything, but shortly after that the labour dispute ended and we were back at work. Image isn't everything, but it helps. Besides that, remember, Teamsters can do anything.

And that may be a reason the movie industry hires Teamsters for their security. Movie makers worry a great deal about who is watching what they are doing, as well as worrying about protecting the stars and the equipment. With Teamsters parked by their film sets there is no worry.

And it was at just such a film set and with just such security that we saw the Teamsters trying to fix a flat tire. No problem, Teamsters can do anything.

"I have no idea how to get this thing off."

That was brother Brett, who was under the minivan.

"The instructions say you remove latch A, which holds cover B, and then slide cover B to the front while unhooking hooks C and D."

That was brother Trevor, who was on his knees while wearing shorts and reading the manual. See, Teamsters are tough. Kneeling on his bare knees.

"I can't get the latch to move," said Brett. The only thing I could see of Brett was his feet. The rest of the union member was under the van.

"Wait," said brother Trevor. "It says to use attachment 1 to undo latch A."

"So where's the attachment?" came the strong and steady without any hint of frustration or anger in it voice of brother Brett.

Brother Wayne who was standing next to the van said, "Maybe I should call BCAA."

What? A Teamster call for help from a non-Teamster. Never, or at least not yet.

"We have to go through the driver's console to release the tool to get the latch open," said Trevor who was turning pages in the manual.

I spoke, somewhat fearful. I don't want to upset a Teamster under a minivan. He might stand up and say something to me and that would upset the van, and maybe me.

"Teamsters can do anything, right?" I said. That was not meant as a question.

"Just give us a second," said Trevor.

I was thinking this story would be like Charles Dickens. This would be the best of times and the worst of times. The best because of the tragedy of Teamsters needing help, the worst because of what they might say after the story was on the air.

"Here's the attachment," said Trevor who had gone through the console and pulled something that released something that moved something that freed the metal and plastic thing that was used to open the latch that will allow the cover to slide before unhooking the hooks.

"That was easy," said Brett.

In a moment the spare tire was free and the story was done.

"Teamsters can do anything," I said at end of the story, while Brett held up his arm like Rocky at the end of the fifteen rounds of battering.

Of course they can. Just like we all can. I added that because I like it and believe it. Would you like to disagree?

Mother and Daughter and the Hummingbirds

This is really nice. I have to tell you that because that's how I feel when I think about this story.

We were wandering around Strathcona Park looking. It's a good life, wandering and looking here and there.

Two women working in a community garden. That is good enough for me. Actually, that is good enough for anyone whether you are looking or working.

This was in the very early spring when most gardeners aren't yet in the garden. There were mother and daughter and they were planting lots of things that would bloom in the summer. Their garden was a few steps from the street where delivery trucks passed every few minutes.

The trucks were going to the produce warehouses along Malkin Street. If you have never been there it is an experience. Basically everything you eat stops off at little Malkin Street on its trip from California to your grocery store. It's a busy place.

And across the street from the community garden is both the food bank and the city's animal pound. One of those is very busy. That, of course, is the food bank, which has turned into an industry, which is both good and bad. Good because it is feeding people. Bad because it has to feed people, but also bad because you cannot believe some of the cars that park across the street and then get loaded with food. Some of them are very expensive cars.

There is no need to prove a need to get food here, and that is good for those who need and don't want others to know about it. I was once one of them. However, it's bad that you can cut your grocery bill pulling up in your BMW and loading the trunk. It is like people who park in disabled parking zones and then get out and walk into the mall. They have disabled signs in their windshields, but they are for other members of the family, not the son or daughter who fills the space while they shop for beer.

I am sorry. Again I digress, but the growth of the food bank is one part of charity I don't understand. The more you give the more need there seems to be. Which came first?

I know some will hate me for that, but as I said, I was there. In any event, it is an industry and the street is always busy.

At the end of the street is the dog pound, the Animal Control Shelter. This is another place that once had an open door for reporters. In this one place I did stories of the blind dog that was adopted by the people who work there, the chicken that escaped from the slaughterhouse off Powell Street and the fellow in his motorized wheelchair who drove from the West End to the East Side every day to walk unwanted dogs. He would attach the leash to his chair on wheels and take them for strolls.

I hate to tell you this next part, but these stories are real. I had gotten to know him fairly well. One day when he was leaving the underground parking in his apartment building in the West End his wheelchair somehow overturned, the gate came down on his neck and he was strangled to death.

That is why I hate to tell you. It hurts, even ten years later. Almost every part of life has the same two ingredients: good and bad, yin and yang, love and hate. Life is not for the faint-hearted.

Those are stories I got from the pound, but then the new rules came out and they are not allowed to talk to reporters without formal consent from headquarters. So no more stories—sad.

The story about the mother and daughter doing the gardening across the street from the pound and the food bank and with trucks going by almost constantly was wonderful. A study in contrasts that cameraman Peter Bremner shot so well.

The mother and daughter were nice, sweet, wonderful. What more could I want? Mother Gloria, daughter Sandy. They were talkative and enthusiastic and friendly and knew a lot about gardening. Can't ask for more.

And that was the story. As I have said, it doesn't take much. They were like chocolate chip cookies for the spirit.

Spring turned into summer and summer was getting late and I was back. Actually I am back there every week but sometimes it takes two seasons to find something, or five months for things to grow.

We were at the same garden with the mother and daughter. Their plants had grown to a beautiful fullness. Hummingbirds were slurping up the sweetness. Most of the world, at least my world, has never seen a hummingbird hovering over a flower and drinking or licking or whatever they do to the nectar deep inside. Talk about miracles. Everything in the garden was alive with colour and movement.

"There is something we didn't tell you last year," said Sandy, the daughter.

"When you last saw us my mother was dying. She had pancreatic cancer. She didn't think she would make it through the spring. She was on heavy chemo."

What? What reserve. What self-control. What lack of self-pity not to tell us earlier. What human beauty. What wonderfulness.

"And now?"

"All better."

And what about Sandy?

I didn't notice when we first met because there was nothing to compare her with, but she weighed just 90 pounds and she didn't think she was going to make it to see the flowers bloom either.

I don't know what her problem was. I didn't ask and she didn't say but she did say she got a life-saving operation. Since then she had gained 45 pounds and was doing well.

Her mother showed us the peas and tomatoes she was growing for her grandson. Near them a hummingbird was drinking from flowers. We were taking pictures of it, beautiful pictures that showed a miracle of nature.

But of course you can see the line coming now; the real miracle was a mother and daughter. You know it if you have ever thought about it: the beauty of a garden is mostly in the gardeners.

The Tree in the Hallway

It lives most of the year in a box. It is forgotten about, ignored. Not even a passing glimmer of thought gets dropped on it.

Then somewhere around the second week of December someone says, "Where did we put that box? It's time, right now."

And someone else says, "You do it. I'm too busy."

And then someone, actually it is Delores Laszuk, the chief editor, says she will get it and a few minutes later the old brown cardboard box comes out of the back of someplace only she remembers and, what do you know? It's Christmas.

"So where are the decorations?" someone else asks.

And Delores opens a drawer that only she remembers is where and, what do you know? It's time to dress the tree.

"Can't do it now," says someone who is standing next to the tree. "Got to cut a story for noon."

It is ten minutes to twelve. No rush. Editors are like that. They live on not panicking even when anyone in their right mind would melt in fear of a hand on a clock that does not stop moving.

"Someone will do it," says Delores who knows that before the short hand on the clock reaches one and the anchors in the next room say goodbye to the audience the tree will be top-heavy with lights and decorations from many years ago.

For the first ten minutes the tree is bare. We are talking about something only as tall as your arm. It doesn't matter how tall your arm is, the tree is the same height. It stands on a small table that wasn't there ten minutes ago.

Then Sabrina Gans looks out through the half-open door of her edit room. She is working on a story that will go on the air before the bottom of the hour. She has pictures of her son and daughter in front of her. They are Rhys and Emily, aged nine and six, and behind her is a calendar with their pictures on each month.

If Sabrina looks in front of her she sees her children. If she turns around she sees her children. There are no wrong directions in her life.

She is part of a mostly young group of editors, all of whom think they are older. She has a husband, her two kids (one of whom is collecting rocks), a new home, visiting in-laws, a clogged rain gutter on her roof and groceries to get this afternoon. That's enough to make anyone think they have lived through everything. And she is right, until the rest comes.

There is soccer on rain-soaked weekends, baseball on sun-baked weekends, and her husband takes the kids fishing in creeks and ponds whenever that is in season, which is all the time.

As far as time and space go for a young family, there is never enough space for all the time that is needed, which makes it a wonderful time. That is the way she will remember it much later when there is more time than is needed for anything.

And on top of all her woes there is the tree just outside her door. She leaves her magic keyboard, takes the string of lights out of the box and spreads them around the stubby plastic branches. She steps back. She moves them. That is what editors do. They rearrange until things look good.

Then she plugs the end of the wire into the socket and instantly—life.

She slides open the glass door to her little room and goes back to moving around the pictures of the story that will be on the air in eight minutes. Not even a nudge up in blood pressure.

Across the hallway is Kim Crillo. She has a two-year-old daughter—Micky, short for Michelina—whom she beams about.

Kim's husband is a professional drummer in a band. Now, in your entire life, how many drummers have you known? Me, none. Kim, one.

Her daughter has her own practice set. I get to see how she is doing when Kim says, "Micky goes like this, and then this," and Kim's hands are beating a rhythm on the edge of the computer. Mother imitating daughter with pride only a mother knows.

This is better than the stories on the air.

At one year Micky was counting. You know that. You've been there. At one year and one month Micky was writing. Micky is basically organizing the household and plotting her future. At one year and a half she is reorganizing the world. At two she is a drummer with her own kit, just like Daddy, only with kid-sized sticks.

It is so good to work with someone with a new child. Kim sees promise and life and fulfillment and beauty in everything. All she has to do is close her eyes and look at her baby or, to be more honest, she takes out her phone and shows us the pictures. People like that make beautiful stories.

She isn't the only one with new babies in the newsroom. Another editor, Ryan Prevost, has a smile as broad as the brim of his baseball cap. His new baby's name is Accalia. No, I'd never the heard the name either. It is from Roman mythology and is derived from the name of the woman who adopted the twins who had been suckled by a she-wolf, Remus and his brother Romulus, the founder of Rome. That is one powerful name. According to those who know such things, people with this name have a deep inner desire to create and express themselves, and they enjoy life immensely.

I'll say it again and again; it is so good to work with happy people.

The opposite is another lesson in philosophy. If the person working with you is an idiot and is always unhappy, you be happy. He or she will either change for the better or report you to human resources as impossible to work with. In either case you win.

When you get older, hearing someone with a new baby is gold.

How much does that shape the news you see? Plenty! When you have a good spirit doing something, the something that comes out is good. I know I am repeating myself again, but some things are worth repeating.

If you are an employer, think of that the next time you groan when you hear that someone working for you is pregnant. It may take a while to get her back, but what you will get is something human resources can't deliver.

If you are an employer, get to know who is in the pictures on the walls of your employees. They will affect your profits. One compliment and the profits would rise.

Now back to the tree in the hallway.

(Please don't expect a chronological flow in these stories. The stories, like everything, are like life. They bounce around. Also, obviously, I like editors. I think they more than most others keep out the bad and suggest the good.

But the fundamental rule of editing is continuity. You must have it, according to the schools of news and movies and books. On the other hand, one of the wisest editors I have ever known said simply, "Continuity is for wimps."

Do what you think is right, and don't break under the rules.)

So, as I was saying, back to the tree in the hallway.

Jeannine Avelino in the next room picks up a tiny dangling ding-dang and hangs it on the tree. Jeannine is in love. Somewhat with her cat and majorly with her boyfriend whom she met long ago, separated from and then got back together with. She has pictures of her cat and her boyfriend in her room. She has stepped out of her room on her way to a run during her lunch break.

"You run a lot?" I ask.

"I try," she says. Then she goes out in the rain, for an hour.

Jump ahead in time.

In the spring I go into the editing room with Kim. She is working days instead of nights. (Don't go into television if you want a normal schedule.)

"I'm working for Jeannine," she says. "She's in Paris running through the streets."

"What?" I say.

This leads to a conversation, as most things do.

"Four years ago," says Kim who has the new baby, "I was a runner. Jeannine came out with me one day. She barely made it to the corner."

Then Kim chooses a picture for today's story. It is a strange one about a little girl naming her knapsack Who-Who. The story is the best part of my day.

First there is the three-year-old girl whose backpack has an owl on it so she calls it Who-Who. Sensible.

Second in the story is one of God's eventual angels. We were told in Sunday school you never know who is an angel. He might be that man dressed in rags. In Sunday school that made me think.

Of course I'm older now. This fellow is covered with tattoos. We know this because he has on no shirt, and the ink is everywhere from stomach to back and arms and neck.

Kim the editor said, "Looks homemade." Editors know everything.

Some of the tats are girls' names with hearts around them. (Yes, the apostrophe is *after* the s, which means plural, as you know.)

He is stretched out on the ground next to his bicycle, which he bought, he says, and on the back tire are many names. Names of his friends and names of his girlfriends. We know they are girlfriends because they have hearts next to them.

"She loves me," he said. "And this one loves me."

This doesn't go over well with his new girlfriend, who is stretched out on the ground next to him.

"Are you jealous?" I ask of her.

"Yes," she says honestly, but then she adds wistfully, "I hope I'll be there soon."

This is something I don't understand. The guy is a loser. The Sunday school teacher would say "If he was an angel he would at least pretend to be nice."

The guy, in my humble, street-educated opinion, hasn't done much to further the advancement of human kind.

Yes, I am prejudiced. Yes, he looks like a schmuck and a nasty schmuck and a bum. At least to me he looks that way but the pretty girl next to him is in love or fascination or delirium.

I have seen this so many times and I can only say, "Girls, smack yourselves in the head and wake up. Schmucks who look like schmucks and act like schmucks are schmucks. You just schmuck yourself when you go with them."

If you look up schmuck in a dictionary—that's an old-fashioned book with words in it—you will see many meanings. All of them are bad or worse but the simple definition of *schmuck* is someone who puts other girls' names with hearts on his bicycle tire and his arms when he goes out with someone else. Also a schmuck is someone who will not pass the Sunday school teacher's test.

Anyway, we had pictures of the names on his bicycle tire and we had the name of a knapsack. Just one more magical ingredient is needed.

And look! Over there is a woman painting a picture. She has a beach umbrella on a pole over her head and her easel in front of her and, wow, she is doing something.

She tells us about the different shades of colour that she is using. It isn't just red and blue; it is carnelian red and cerulean blue.

I love people who use long names. I don't want to be with them or be friends, I just want to hear them use long names because that is like a CBC newscast. I don't know what they are talking about but I feel like I have learned something afterwards.

Together the little girl with the backpack, the soon-to-rise angel with the names on his bike tire and the artist make a story.

I honestly don't know how, but we can work on it.

That is the same with all things. Whatever you get dealt, just work on it.

Remember Kenny Rogers's song "The Gambler": every hand's a winner and every hand's a loser. That is another bit of eternal advice that should be taught in Harvard or Yale. We got it free in a song.

Whatever you get, work with it. It's better than complaining you got a bad hand, throwing down your cards and feeling sorry for yourself.

We have a three-year-old with a backpack and an artist and a schmuck, and we're working on it in Kim's tiny editing room.

"Funny," she said, looking at Jeannine's dark room, "Jeannine could barely run back then. But she took it up with everything she had. She trained and ran and now—a marathon."

"What?" as I said a few pages ago.

Then I added, "Paris?!"

Kim smiled as though she were the parent of a marathoner.

Kim was so proud of her friend. She took her jogging once and there was born a long-distance runner. Jeannine's boyfriend went with her when she ran in Paris. She is happy. Again, the work that happy people do has that look about it. You can't buy it. You can only appreciate it.

And then, because this is reality and this is how things work, we went back to the story of the backpack and the owl.

I keep saying it, but don't worry if you don't have a plan for getting somewhere. Just go, and you will get there. And that will be the best place.

The story turned out to be beautiful. Just a little girl talking about her backpack.

Kim was happy. She got to talk about her friend and her baby. And I was happy. I got to work with people who were happy.

It sounds so trite, but it is not. The stories in everyone's lives are the best. And usually, the rewards will be better than the project you are working on.

Take a breath. We're going back to the tree. (Sorry if you prefer the shorter stories of the past books. They were about the stories that are my life. These, the longer stories, to be honest, are about my life wrapped up in the stories. It is hard to tell them apart.)

And then there is Derek Whelan. He is one of the two, or two-and-a-half, who are not young, but he is a writer and he is Irish, so he is double blessed. He edits in the day and writes at night.

He doesn't say he is Irish because his great-grandfather came from Ireland. Derek is from there himself, which makes him really Irish, and almost everyone in Ireland wants to be a writer because how else can you suffer and go through anxiety and pain and despair and struggle unless you are a writer?

To be Irish you must be a writer. Ireland doesn't produce many artists, despite being in such a beautiful country, but it pours out writers, some of the most incredible in the history of the world. And there are no light, happy writers. Dr. Seuss would have died in a pub in Ireland.

Derek is one of Ireland's writers, living in Canada, looking for a publisher.

He is very good. He is deep and lyrical and meaningful and touching and sometimes he gives up Guinness just to write, which is a sacrifice only those in Ireland would understand. When I listen to him he is a writer in all the categories that are Irish.

On his father's eightieth birthday he went back to Ireland to read a letter he had written for him. He hired a violist to play while he read.

"Did he like it?" I asked.

"I don't know, but everyone else did," he said.

Derek walked by the tree. He always wears a white shirt and tie, sometimes a bow tie. In the spring he came to work with a white jacket and cane. He is a writer.

But today he picked up a decoration and put it on a branch near the top and then kept on walking.

In the next two rooms are Corinne Newell and Ashley Alonzo.

They get up at three a.m., they have coffee and stale cake from yesterday for breakfast at four a.m. and the first things they see are accidents and death.

That is when the rest of us are sleeping. They put the death here and the day there. Try that every day and keep your sanity.

They leave for home when the rest of the world is having lunch.

But on their way down the hallway they each take a decoration out of the box and put it on the tree.

And further down the hall is Carl Waymen, who lost 80 pounds of himself when he went on a diet. It was simple. He just ate less. He drank less. He ate better. He walked. Try it. No gimmicks, no rules, no counting of calories or weighing of portions. You got fat by eating too much, drinking too much and moving too little, so eat less, drink less and move more. It works. Guaranteed.

He has no belief in a god—he thinks religions have caused many of the wars of the world—but he looked at the tree at the end of the hallway.

"Nice," he said.

Ethan Faber walked by. Assistant news director. Management. Not an editor. He stopped, picked up a decoration and hooked it on the tree near the bottom, which was bare. Good for him.

He started to walk away, stopped, turned, came back and put on a second decoration.

Okay, management has a heart.

Greg Novik was at the end of the hallway and he has recently retired. Everything is always changing. That is another rule of life. Right after you say "Nothing's new," hang on. In a moment everything will be. There is a philosophical truth in there. I only wish I knew what it was.

He was the oldest of the editors and we had long talks about things such as the meaning of life and editing before computers. One of those, the meaning of life, was easy to understand.

For the Christmas stories I've done for CTV Greg did everything imaginable and more to find pictures of kids on Christmas morning and Santa and also a picture of a tree that looked amazingly like the tree at the end of the hallway.

Only if you write, "'Twas the night before Christmas..." can you get away without using pictures. I didn't write that and Greg saved me.

A few other editors and the tree:

There's James Buck, who gave me the brilliant line at the pond at the end of the PNE story. He put a decoration on the tiny boughs.

He is another person involved with marathons, like Jeannine, but he just goes to them with his wife. She's been in seven. "She runs, I carry the bags and meet her at the finish line," he says.

He also knows more about baseball than I do, although he was impressed when I told him I saw Jackie Robinson play, once.

And there's Vinh Nguyen, the editor in the Vietnamese immigration story. He opened his door, snatched up a tiny star and put it on the top. Then he closed his door.

In truth, it is 12:45 p.m., the show is still on the air and last-minute stories are still being put together.

Vinh is the one who made everyone cry at his wedding. Less than a year later his wife was pregnant. He ran, well almost ran, through the edit hallway and most of the rest of the newsroom showing everyone an ultrasound picture saying, "My son, my son!" He was truly the happiest man on earth. The same as his stories.

Adam Lee is another newcomer, a newcomer being anyone who came after me. The first time I walked into the room where he was working I saw a baseball on the desk next to his editing computer.

"Why?"

"I like baseball," he answered.

This is going to be the beginning of a beautiful friendship, I thought. I would have told him that line came from *Casablanca* but I figured anyone smart enough to like baseball would know that.

Adam and his wife went to San Francisco for three days, during which they saw two baseball games. They will have a happy life.

Simon DiLaur is another new editor. He came here from

Ottawa because his girlfriend moved here. Right away you know he is a good guy.

We were working together one day when he told me he and his girlfriend were going to New York. He told me all the sights they would see and the things they would do.

I was nodding.

"Have you ever been there?" he asked. We have much to talk about.

It is now one p.m. The show in the next room is over. Deloris, the chief editor, who is truly a mother to all of this group (including Greg, who is older), looked at the tree.

"I knew it," she said.

Deloris is now retired but before she left she passed on the storage location of the tree to James, the new chief editor. It is now a family tradition.

(Now that James is in management he goes to meetings and then more meetings and then more. Meetings take time away from editing, which he is a genius at. If only management knew how to meet less. What they need is a good editor.)

Now the tree was covered with decorations and lights, no longer an artificial piece of old plastic that was packed away for a year. It was a glowing—okay, tiny, but nonetheless welcome—window to Christmas.

How did it get decorated so quickly? The same way those presents appear under the tree on Christmas morning. Someone must have done it.

There is one more visitor down the hallway. Her name is Alex Turner. She is not an editor, she is a writer in the newsroom. Writers are even more unrewarded than editors. All those things you hear the anchors saying come from the minds and fingers of writers in the back, almost literally in the shadows. They spend their working lives turning out story after story after . . . you get the picture.

Try an experiment. Type something on your computer and time how long it took you. Then read it and time that. Writers spend more time writing than readers spend reading—and then the readers get the credit. Television is like life.

Alex is the daughter of an editor with whom I worked long ago. Chris Turner was one of the legends: shirt wrinkled sometimes, hair uncombed usually, coffee cups half-empty always.

This is not criticism. This is praise. He was an artist. He looked like one and he acted like one, oblivious to the world around him, even though that world was one of deadlines and time limits.

What he did was turn out videos that became alive. These were stories about fires and death and storms, proving anything can be made into art, and by the end of each story his shirt was even more wrinkled.

All this makes his daughter an honorary editor, but that is only part of the reason that I mention her here. The other is that she was, as the Bible puts it, with child as she looked at the tree.

It just seemed right.

PS: Like many artists, Chris Turner discovered that living off art is impossible, and he is no longer an editor. The last time I saw him, just a few months ago, not only did I not recognize him but I didn't believe it was him even when he shook my hand. Suit, tie, neat haircut, polished shoes, and if we'd had coffee together I'm sure he would have finished it and it would probably have been a latte. He now sells real estate, but to someone else he will be "My grandfather, the crazy artist."

The Very Brief Meeting

I hadn't noticed him. That's why I almost bumped into the cart of bananas he was pushing.

I was in Walmart. No, I have no prejudices.

"Sorry," I said.

"No, it was my fault," said the man behind the cart.

"No sweat," I said.

He looked at me for a second, maybe recognizing me, maybe not. The look I saw was blankness.

"I'm really sorry," he said. "It's been a bad day. We lost one of our own."

When terrible things happen, when wonderful things happen, the urge to tell someone overpowers the strongest silence.

"I'm so sorry," I said. And then not knowing what else to say I asked, "Was it an accident?"

I was trying to read his name tag but I didn't have on my glasses.

"No, I don't know the cause but he was young."

And then, with the banana cart next to us, he lowered his head and the words came out, first to the floor then to me.

"He was special needs, but he was always so happy. It really hurt all of us."

"What's your name?" I asked.

"Jocomo," he said.

Italian, I thought, but no accent so he was probably born here. There I was, analyzing the only thing I could, but it was the only way to share anything with him.

And then he said, "I was so glad I spoke to him. Pretty often. I said hello a lot and asked how he was."

It was then that Jocomo smiled. He had found a good memory. He had something to hold onto. He and the poor fellow who is no more had a relationship.

If Jocomo hadn't talked to him the death would have been just someone in the store. Because he did talk, the death was personal, and the thought that he had given something of himself to someone else meant that he was part of the other.

That is about the best way I can explain it, because Jocomo could not explain it beyond saying, "I was so glad I spoke to him."

And then he excused himself and went on pushing the cart.

I got out a piece of paper and wrote "Jocomo" on it. I didn't want to forget his name. I wouldn't forget the story.

Going Home

The bucket list for many people says Spain, followed by France, Germany and Italy, or the opposite order. Fred just wanted to see the old porch in east Vancouver, and I was lucky enough to be there when he did.

Now, here are a couple of things in order. Fred Ko is one hundred years old. People who reach that age are getting to be common but it is still an amazing number, especially when you are like Fred.

On his one hundredth birthday, on March 28, 2016, he climbed the front steps of the old, very old, house at 616 Princess Avenue. He climbed the four steps with no cane or support from anyone else.

He said they were wood when he played here. It is concrete now. He said the little girl from across the street and he would play on the porch when it rained.

He looked at the narrow part that was covered by an overhang.

"It looked so big back then."

It always does. We grow, our past shrinks. Under your kitchen table was once a fort, a forest, a spaceship, a hide-out. Now you bang your head if you try to reach under it to pick up a napkin.

You know all this. You know that when you go back to your old neighbourhood you see things that are invisible to those now living there. You see your friends who are gone and the dirt pile that is now paved over and the front steps that were wood and now are concrete.

That is what Fred Ko saw, while a crowd of children and nieces and nephews and their husbands and wives stood on the sidewalk taking pictures of him.

They will look at the pictures and say this is Grandpa, father, Uncle Fred on the porch where he grew up. What their cameras will not get, of course, because even digital cameras don't have souls, is Fred saying, "This is unbelievable."

"I walked to kindergarten."

"You what?"

"I walked to kindergarten."

Kids on the street now are driven there, three blocks away.

Of all the possible birthday presents on earth—a trip to Spain or Hong Kong or even tea at the Empress—none could have been better than going home.

Happy Birthday, Fred.

Steve Saunders

"No, I didn't read it."

"Are you kidding? It's got all the history in it."

Steve Saunders is driving. We are looking.

"I told you about the Grandview ditch, right?" I said as we were approaching the Grandview ditch.

"Yeah, I remember, sort of."

"What do you mean, 'sort of you remember'?"

"It had something to do with a railroad."

"Did you read my book?"

Steve drove over the overpass over the ditch on Victoria and Broadway. It is one of the great wonders of the city.

"No, I didn't read it. Not yet," he said.

"What? That's one of the best stories of the city."

"Well I bought your book, but then I gave it to my in-laws."

"Where are your in-laws?"

"They live downstairs in our house."

I took a deep, deep breath and held it. But you know what happens when you hold your breath.

"You what? Your in-laws have your book and they live in your house and you can't borrow my book?"

"Well, I've been busy."

There you go. Multi-tasking is the ruin of history.

"So a new railroad wanted to come into Vancouver," I started saying, "but the only route was uphill, so they hired some Chinese folks and said start digging and . . . Oh, forget it. Borrow the book."

First, something about Steve. A long time ago he quit his news camera job in Vancouver to move to Australia for an adventure. He was there for several years before he got homesick and came back.

It doesn't matter if that puts you behind in the seniority list. That is the kind of move that lets you see how others see things, and that is one of the greatest lessons in life. Now Steve is writing a screenplay about a murder mystery. Okay, that's one excuse for being busy, but still.

Then I asked if his in-laws still owned their pub?

"No, that was years ago."

Their pub was named after one of the greatest figures in British Columbia: Billy Miner. It makes my heart sad to think I haven't written about him for years and it makes me glad that he is always there to remind me how amazing life can be.

The Billy Miner Pub is just off the Haney Bypass, and not far from the scene of his most historic moment in crime.

First you should know that Billy Miner was a thief, an armed robber, a kind man, an elegant gentleman, a most loved fellow and a prison escapee. I would wish to be like him minus the years in solitary confinement when that meant a freezing concrete floor with no light, no bed, no toilet, no sink and only bread and water when the guards felt like feeding you. That wouldn't fit into Canada's food guide.

It meant having cold water thrown on you and on the floor for sport. It meant beatings for the same reason.

Apart from that he had a great life.

He was American. He robbed stagecoaches when there were stagecoaches and went to prison for doing that. When he got out there were no more stagecoaches so he robbed trains, and one of them was just past Mission on the way to Maple Ridge. It's a fascinating story. Either get the books or I'll tell you it now. Okay.

Well, he got away with stacks of loot, which greatly upset the Canadian Pacific Railway. It wasn't that they lost the money as much as their reputation. They were the carrier of gold and stocks and cash. There was no other way to move it. If one rotten outlaw with the help of a couple of other guys could stop a giant train and escape with the goods, what was the future for the rich people in this country?

So they hired a trainload of private police to track him down. Meanwhile Billy Miner was living in peace in the interior, well protected by the local folks who said he was the nicest, most generous man they had ever known.

Once in a while he went away on a business trip.

After years of more holdups the police caught him, of course, and he went back to prison—this time to the penitentiary in New Westminster, which was surrounded by towering grey walls.

And there he met the warden's daughter. Now as I and everyone said, Billy Miner was a nice guy, in prison only because he made a mistake, and whatever he said to the warden's daughter he clearly didn't appear to her like a hardened criminal.

The short of that was that a ladder was found near the wall that he escaped over. They never caught him. At least not here. The next train he robbed was on the east coast of the US.

He died in prison in the States, but the townsfolk there all put together some money and saved him from being buried in the pauper's ground. He got a beautiful headstone in the city's main cemetery.

How could you not like him? That is a history to be proud of.

And Steve's in-laws ran the Billy Miner Pub, which is almost as good as being on the railroad tracks when he said, "This is a holdup." He never fired his pistol.

Then Steve and I went to Trout Lake and found the little girl with the owl on her knapsack and the guy with the bike tires (but without Billy Miner's heart or intelligence or consideration) and then the artist whose description of colours was, well, artistic. It was a good day for us.

And now I am glad I wrote this book. Thinking about all of you and writing about you—everyone in this book and everyone not in it, not yet—makes me happy, which isn't a bad return for sitting down, closing my eyes and typing what I am thinking. I'm a lucky guy.

But Steve, if you buy this book and give it to your in-laws and they come upstairs and say, "Did you read this?" and you say, "No, too busy," we will have to have a little talk.

Thank you, everyone.
—Mike